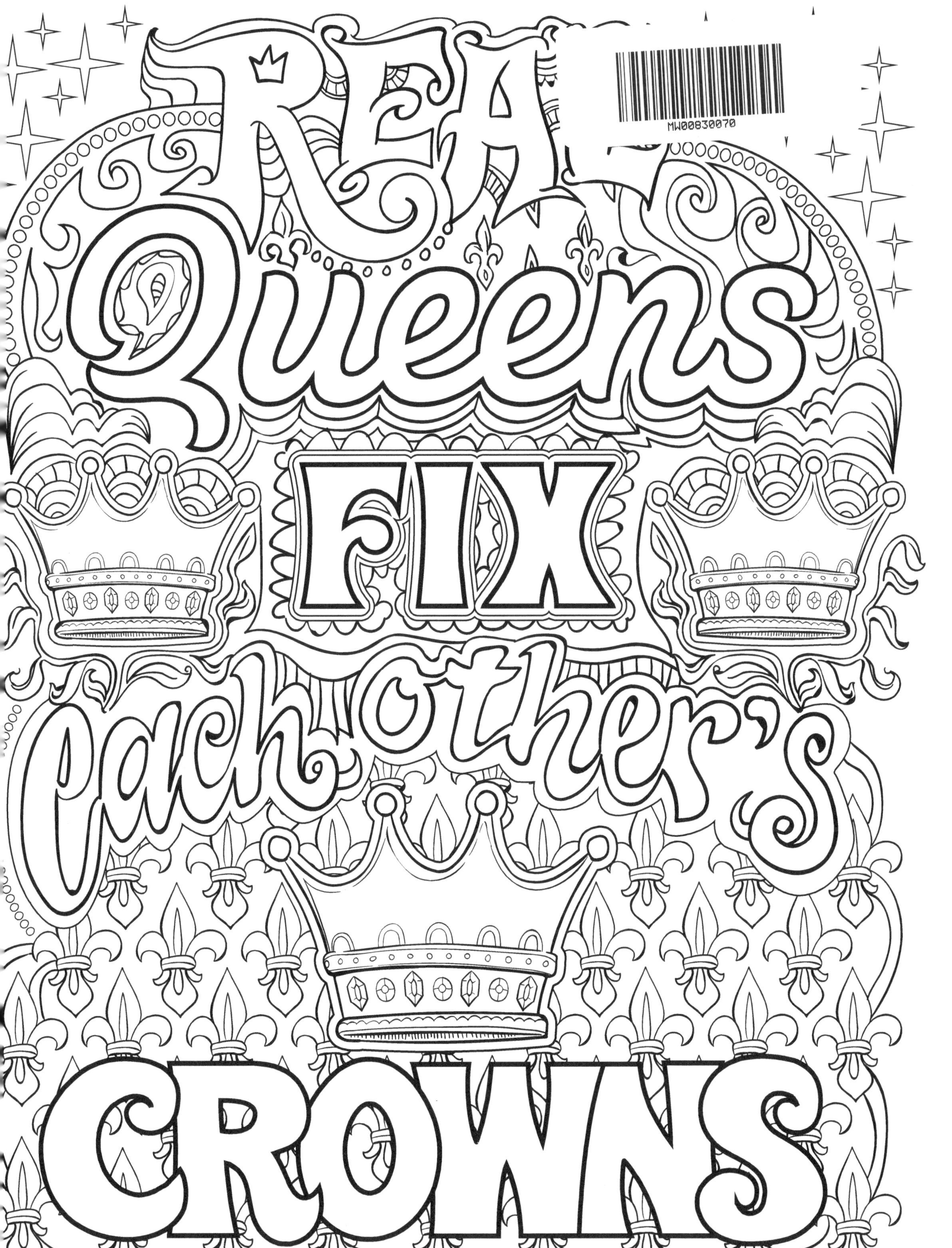
REA
Queens
FIX
each other's
CROWNS

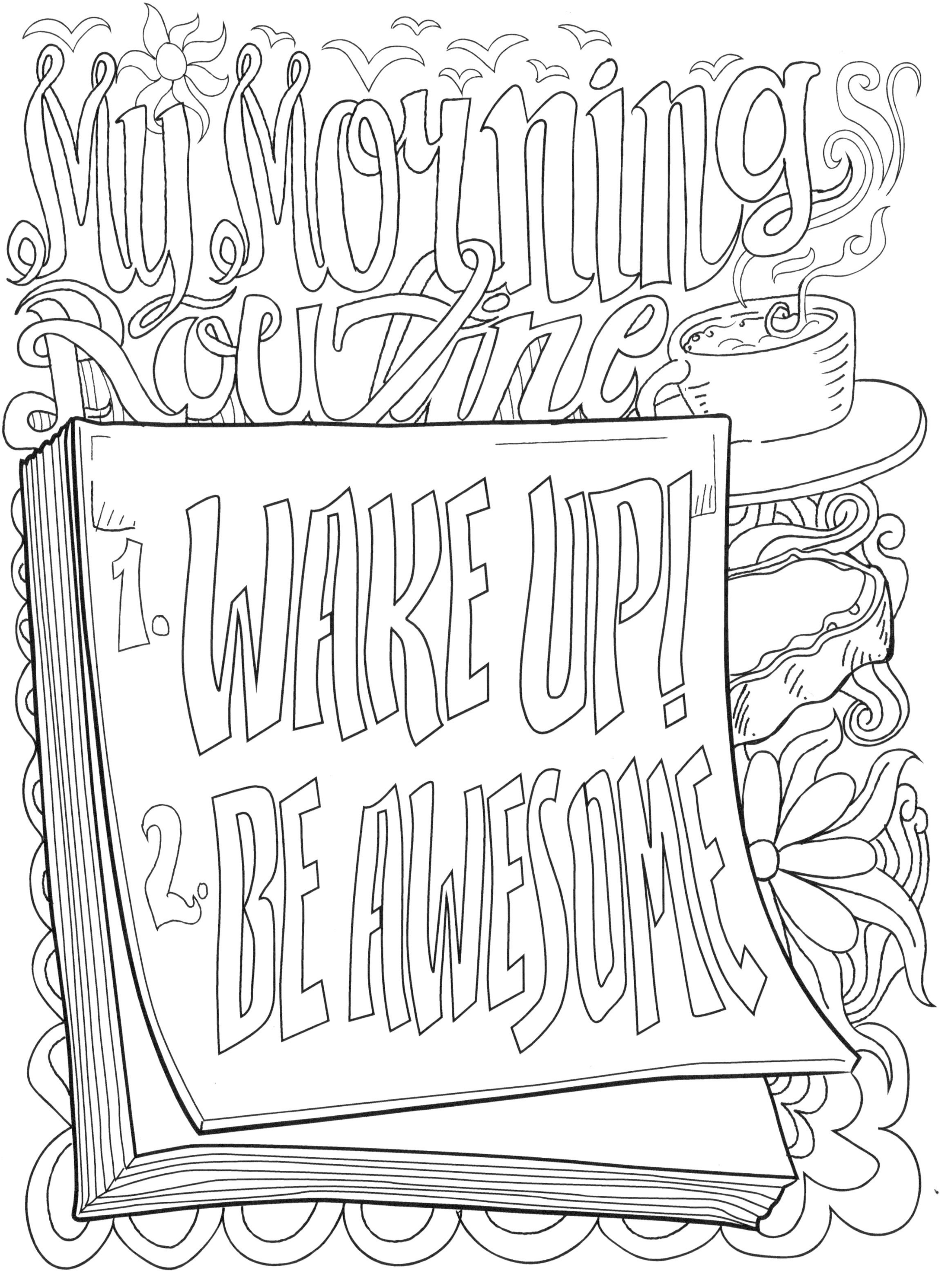
My Morning Routine
1. WAKE UP!
2. BE AWESOME

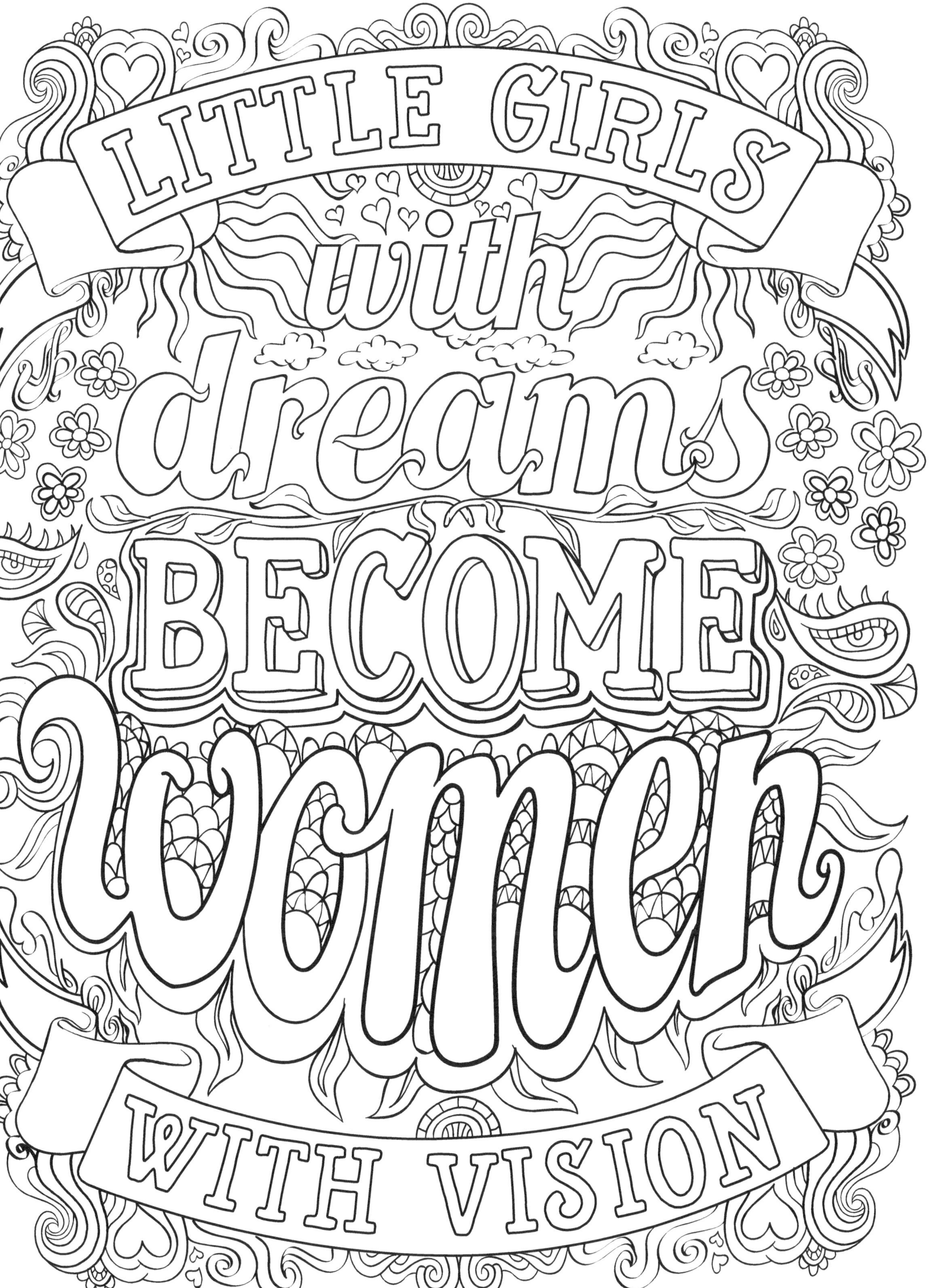
LITTLE GIRLS
with
dreams
BECOME
women
WITH VISION

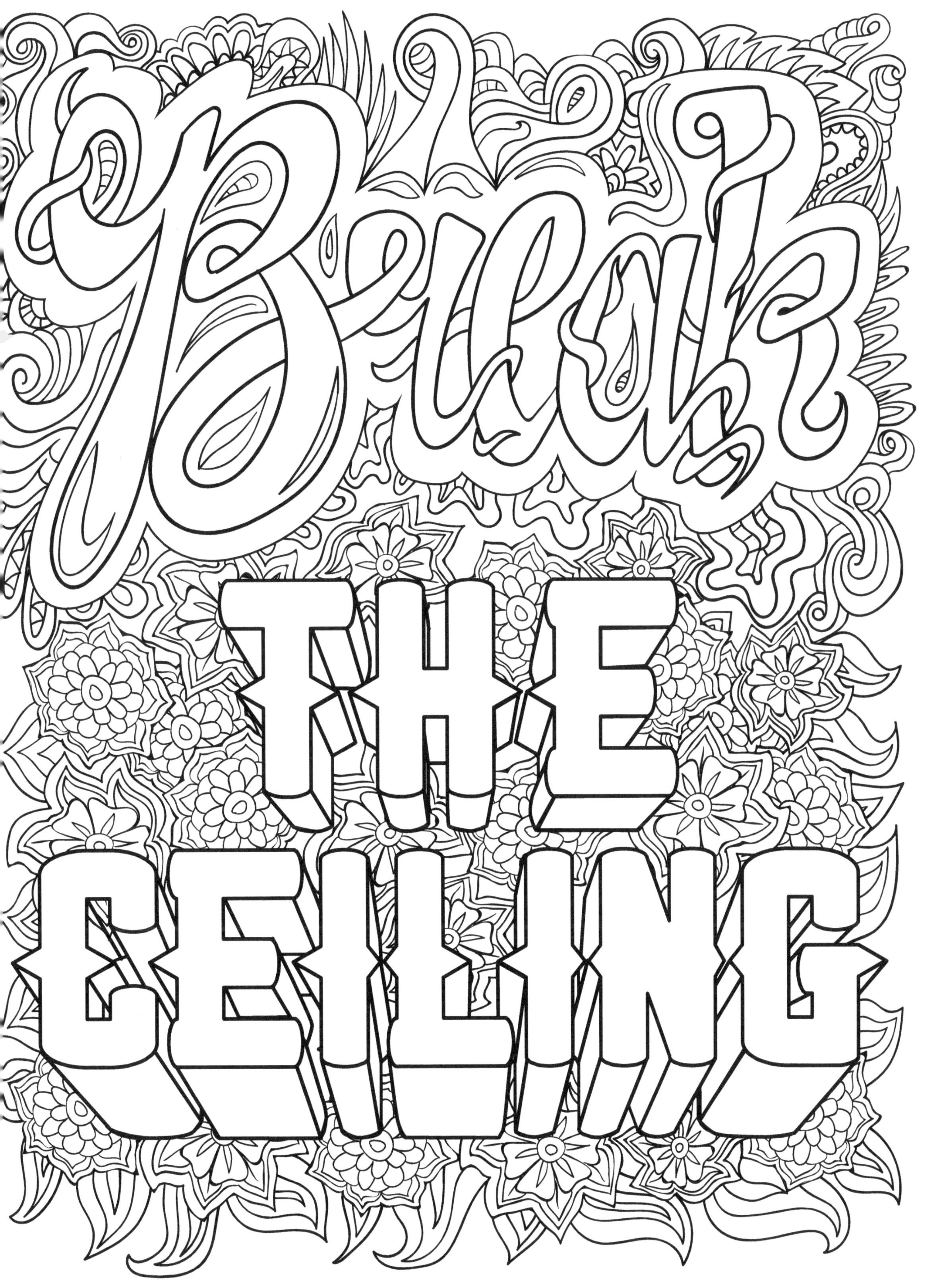
Break
THE
CEILING

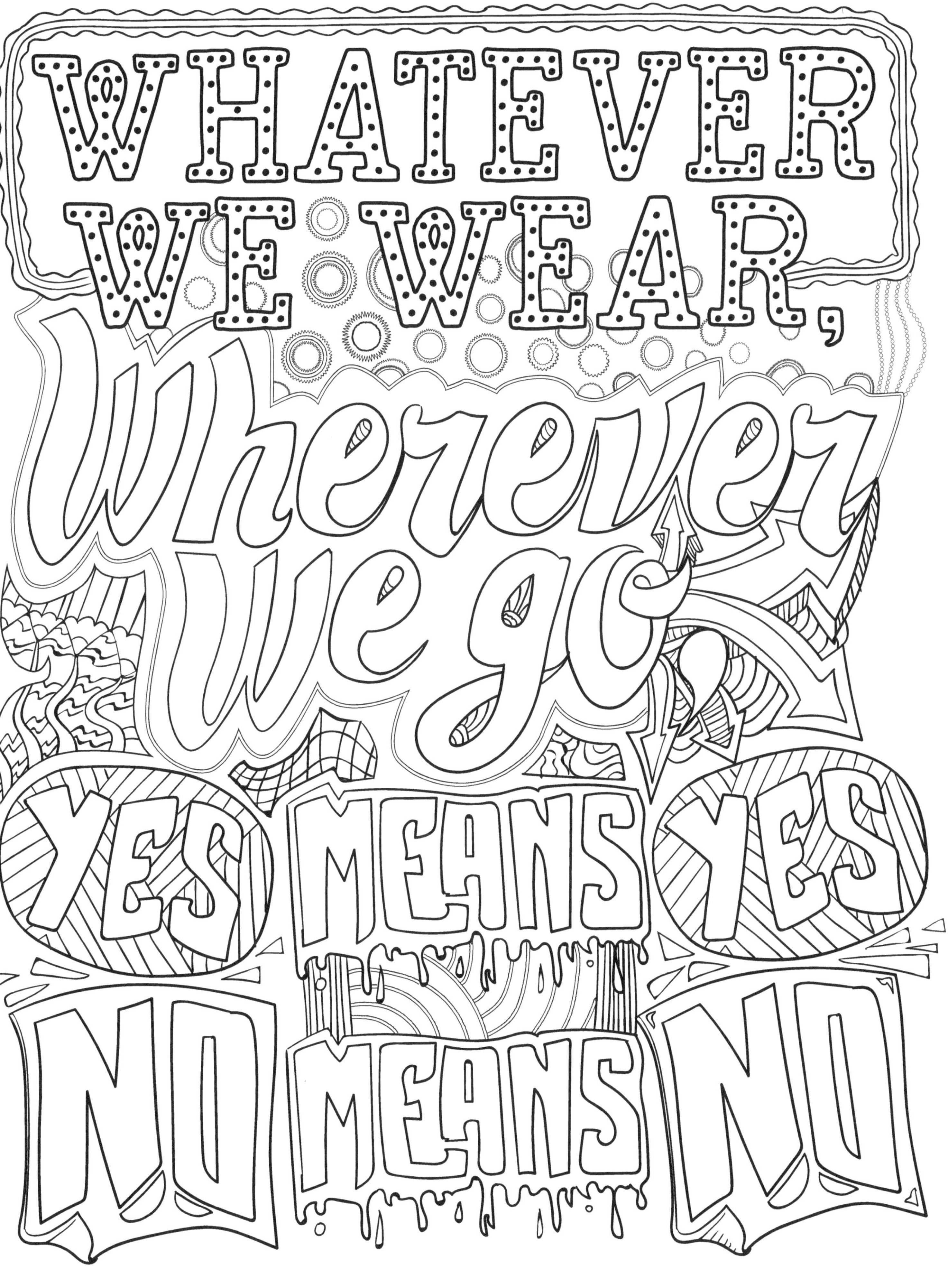
WHATEVER WE WEAR,
Wherever we go,
YES MEANS YES
NO MEANS NO

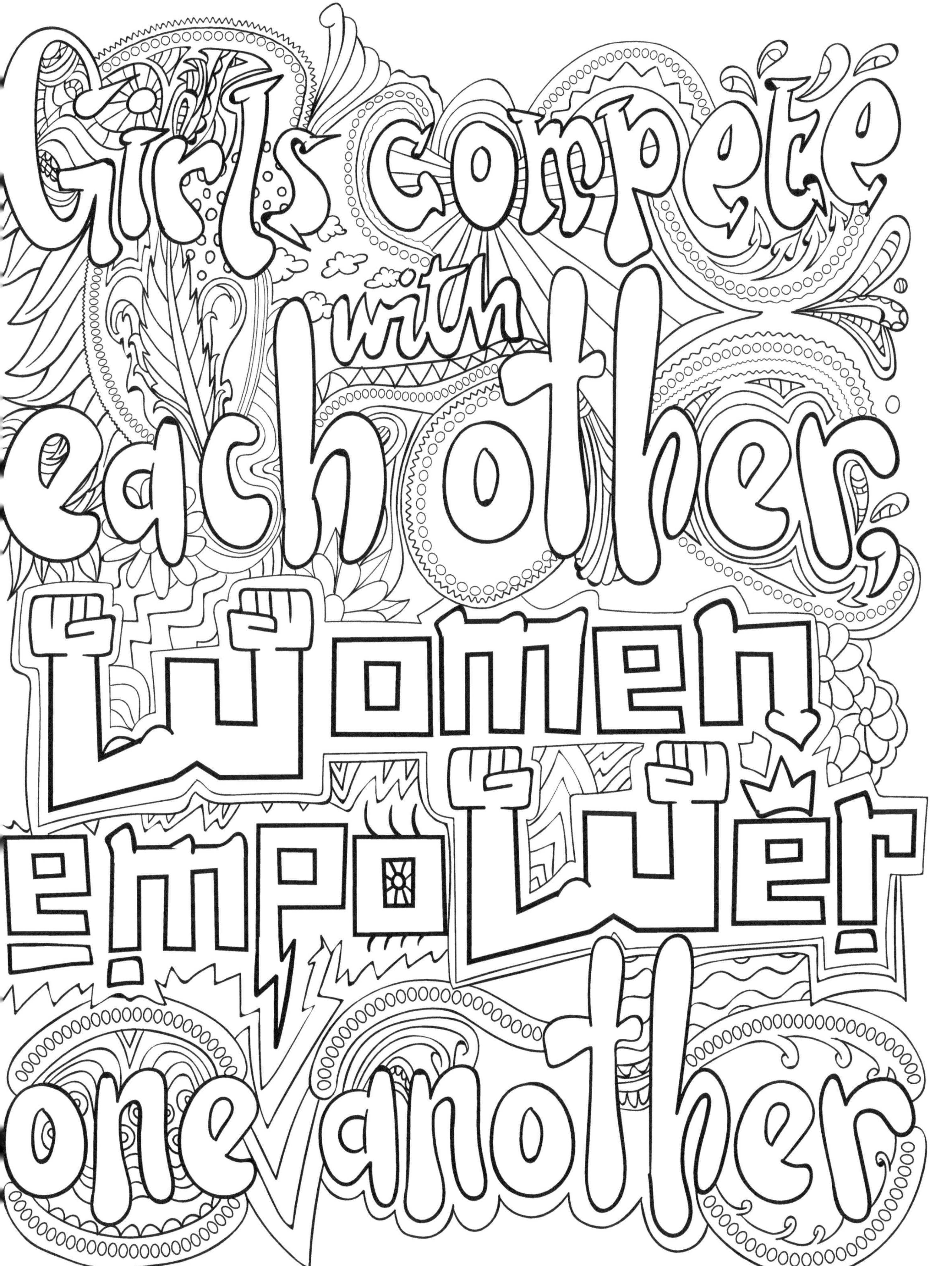
Girls compete with each other,
Women empower one another

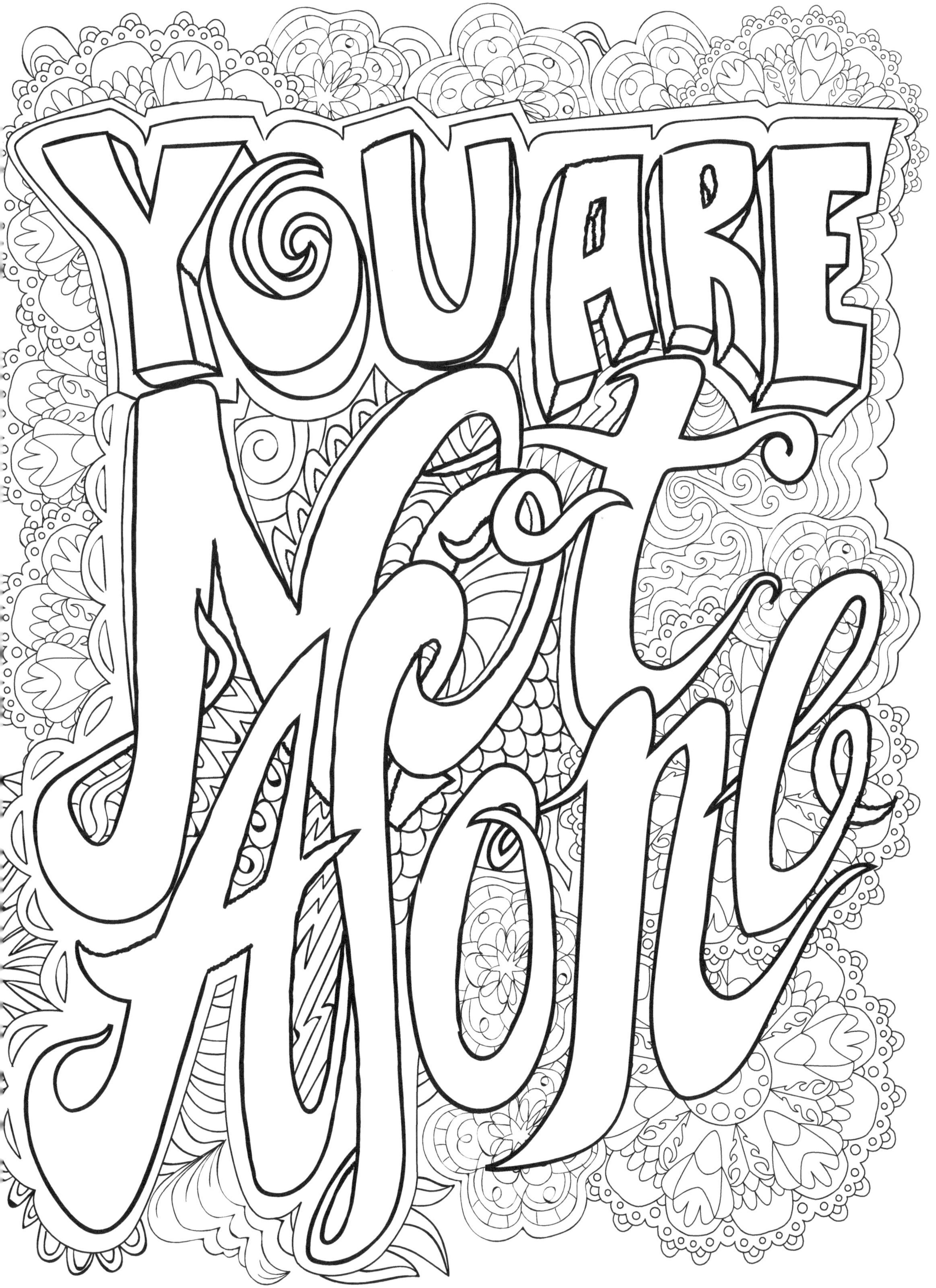
YOU ARE

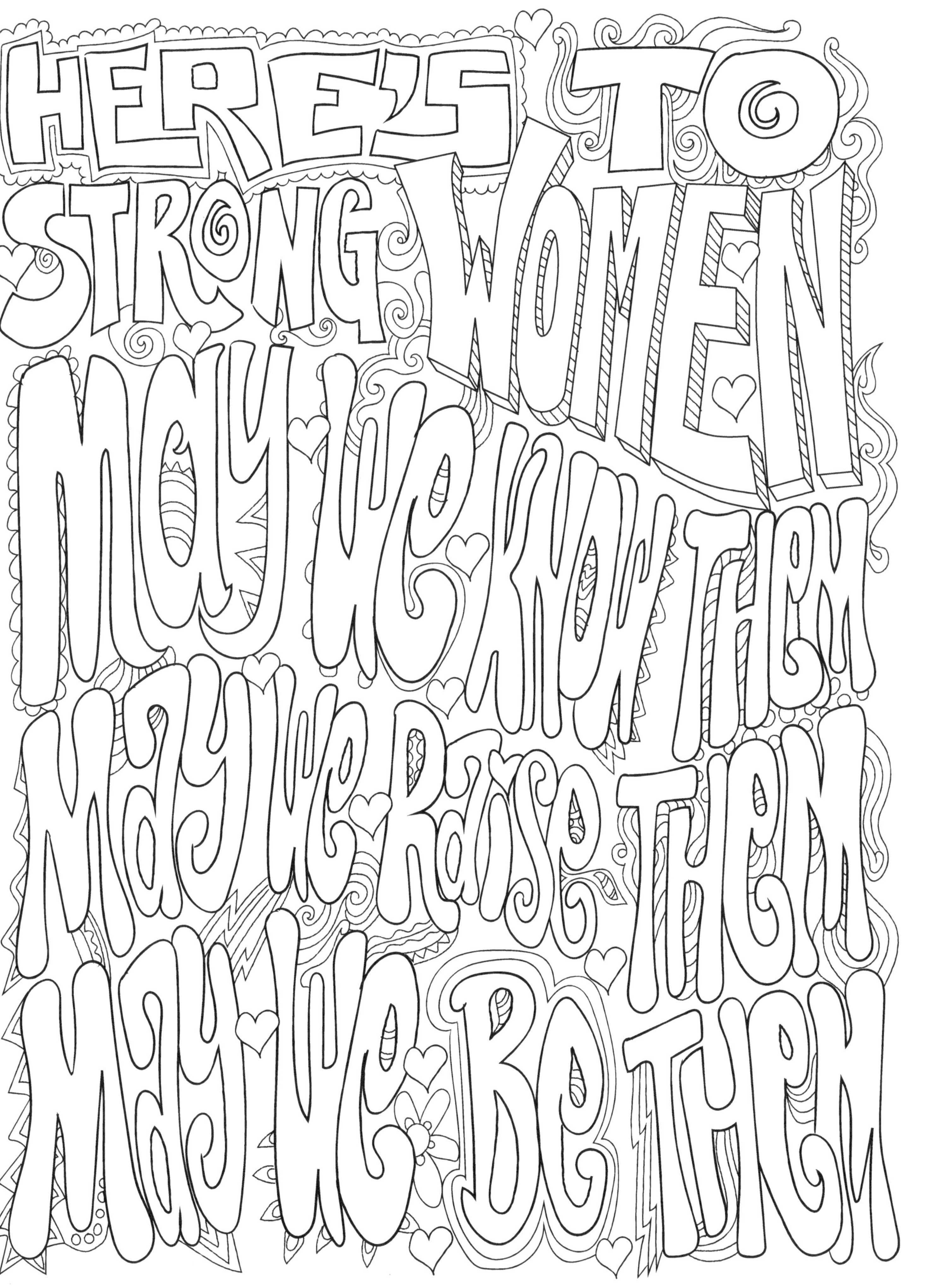
HERE'S TO
STRONG WOMEN
MAY WE KNOW THEM
MAY WE RAISE THEM
MAY WE BE THEM

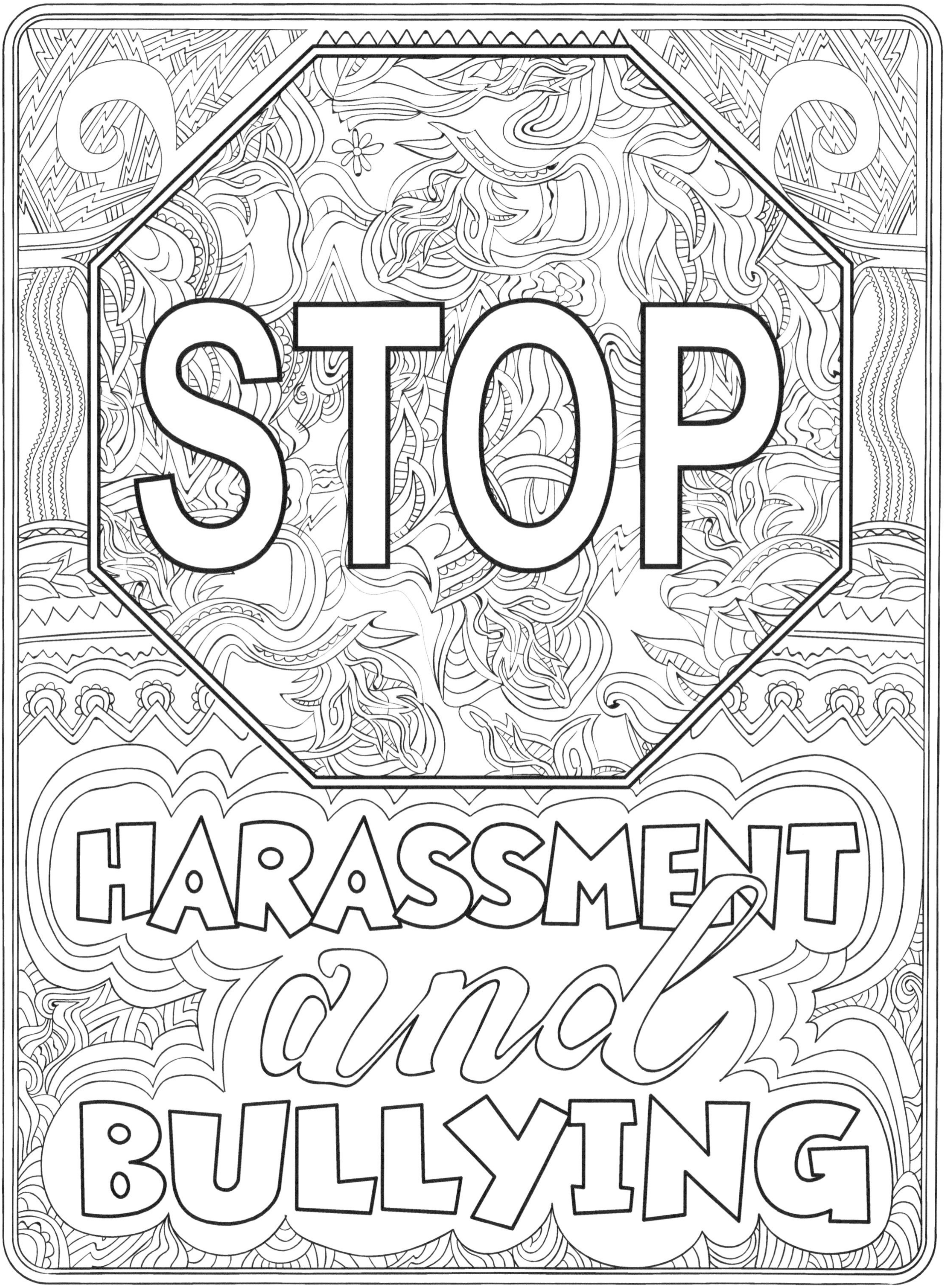
STOP
HARASSMENT
and
BULLYING

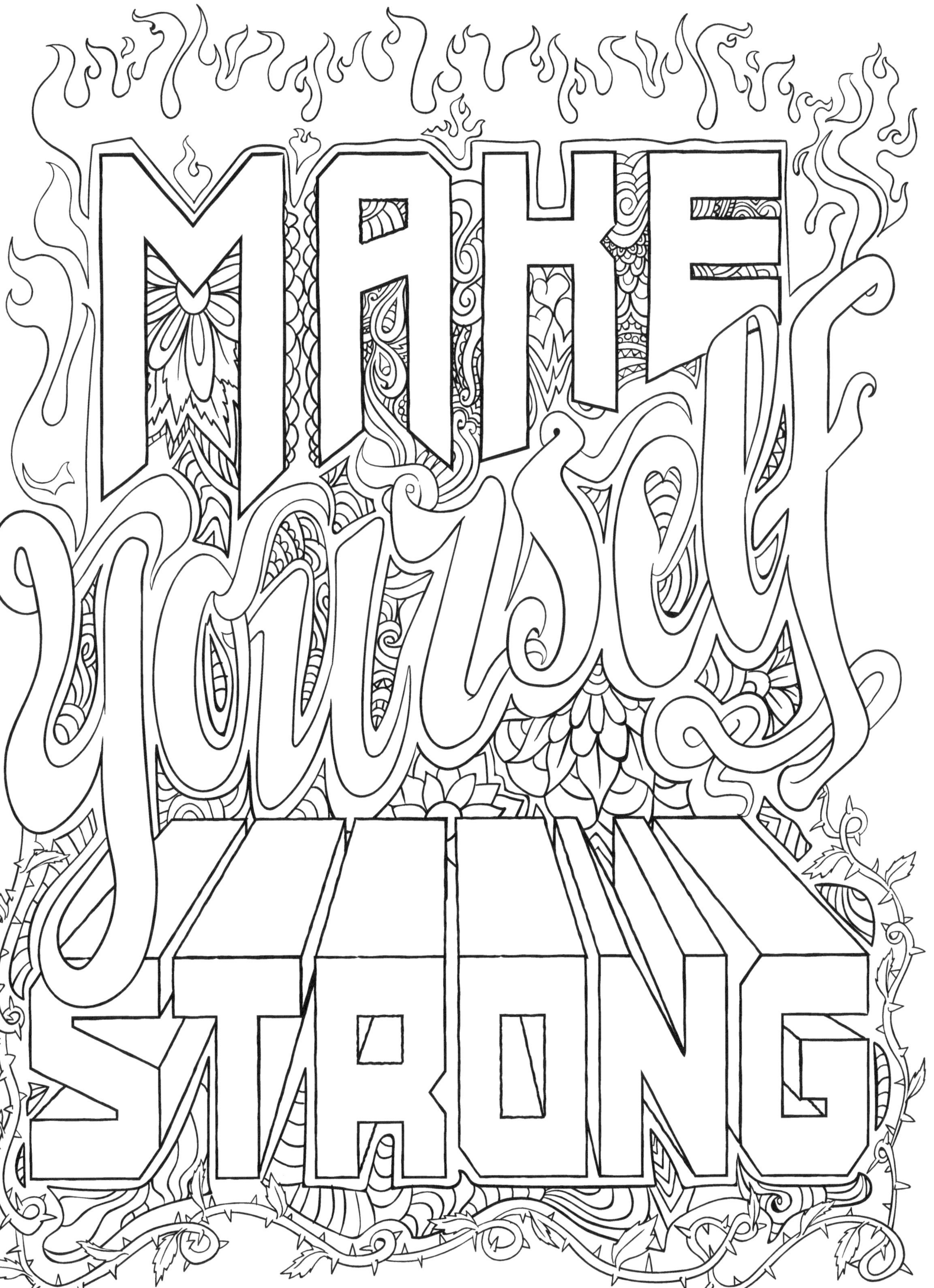
MAKE
yourself
STRONG

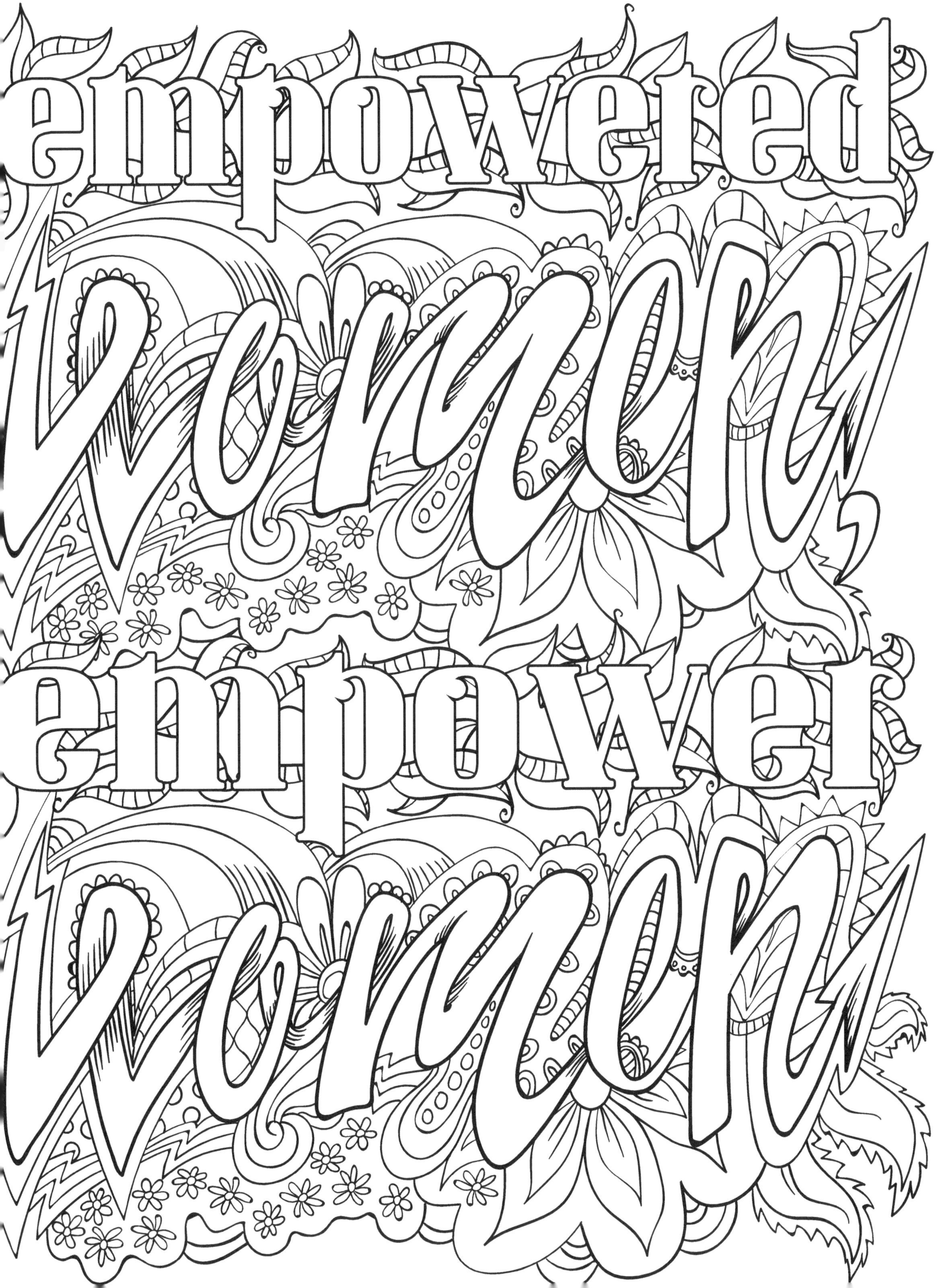
empowered
women
empower
women

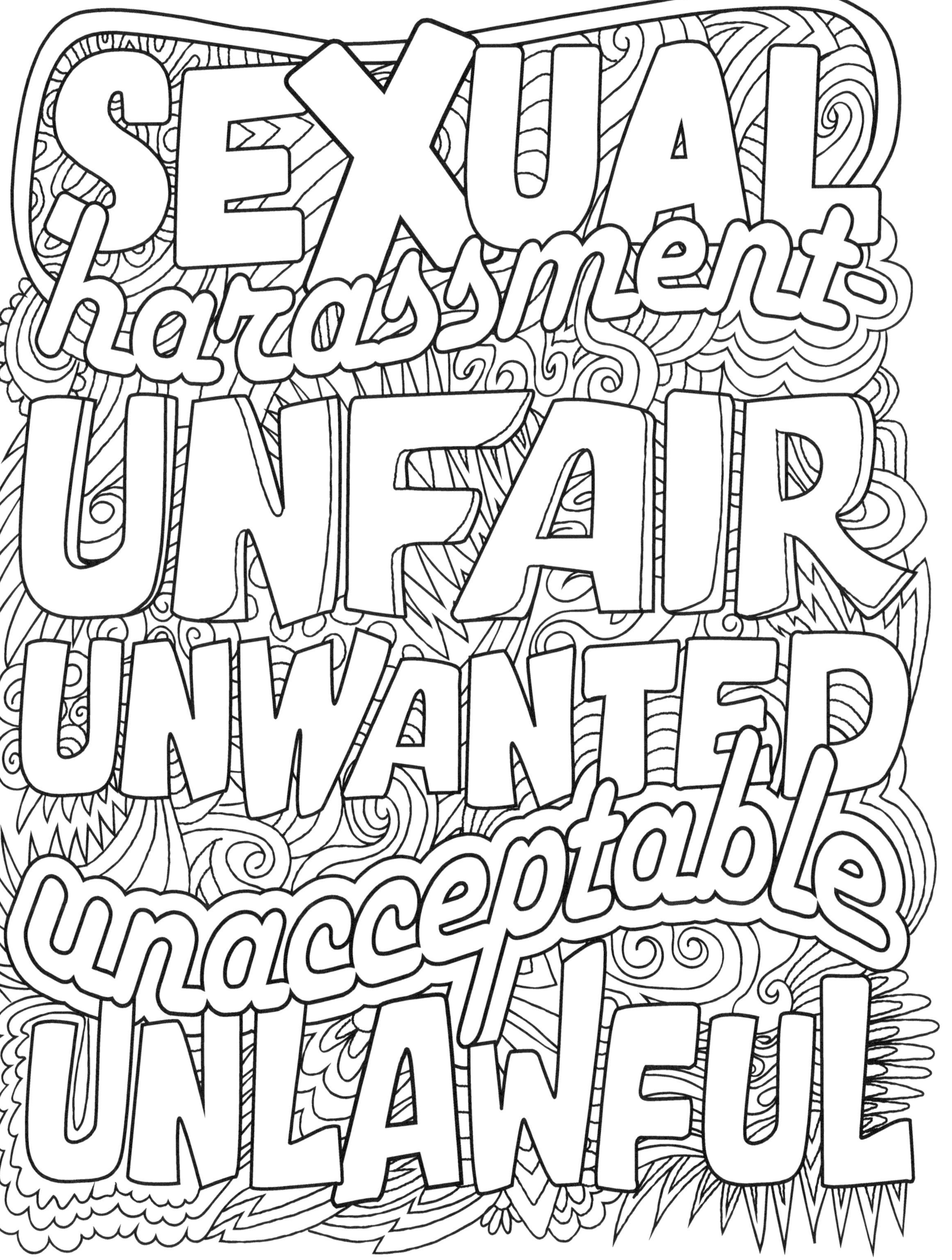
SEXUAL
harassment-
UNFAIR
UNWANTED
unacceptable
UNLAWFUL

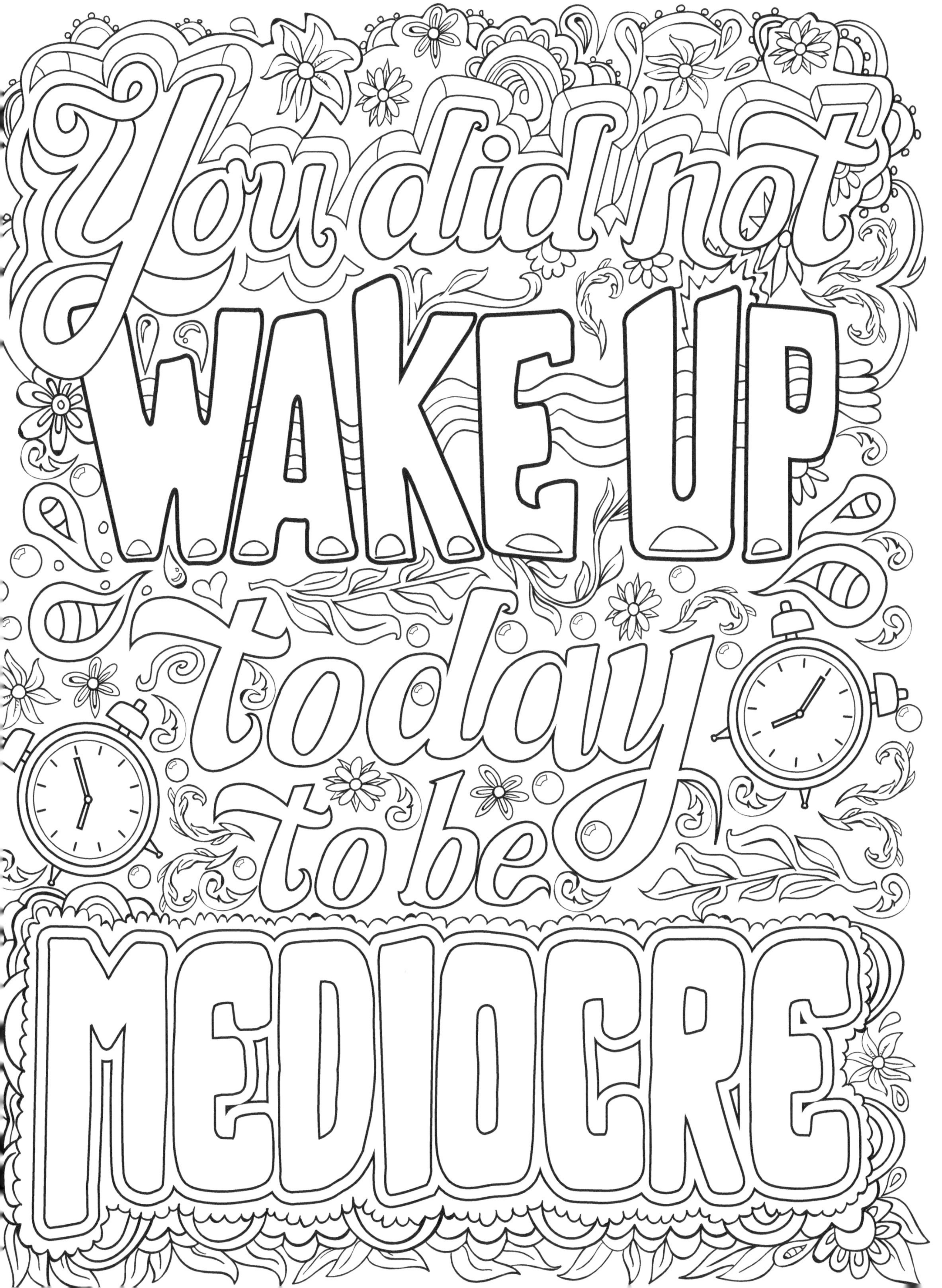
You did not
WAKE UP
today
to be
MEDIOCRE

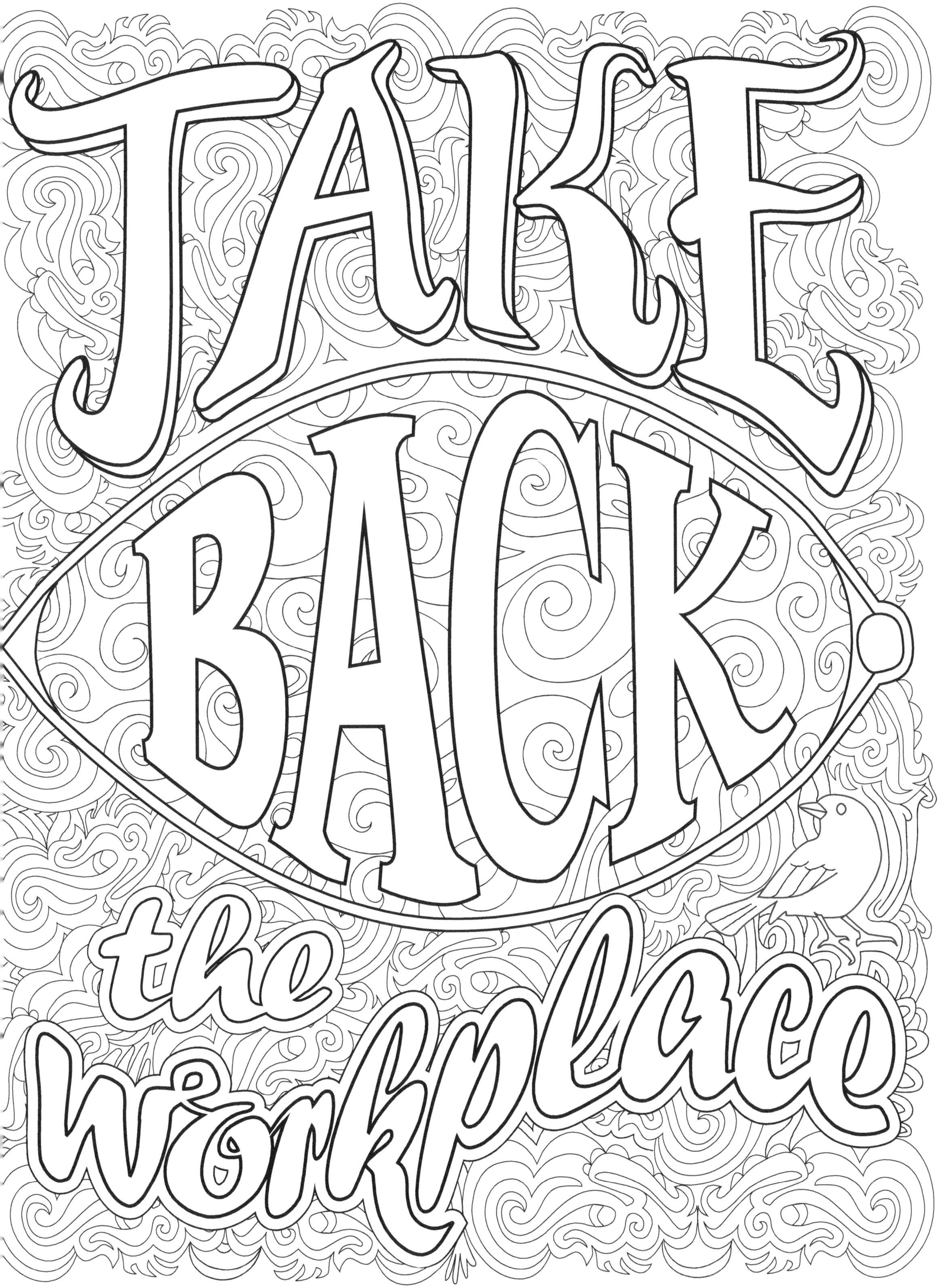
TAKE
BACK.
the workplace

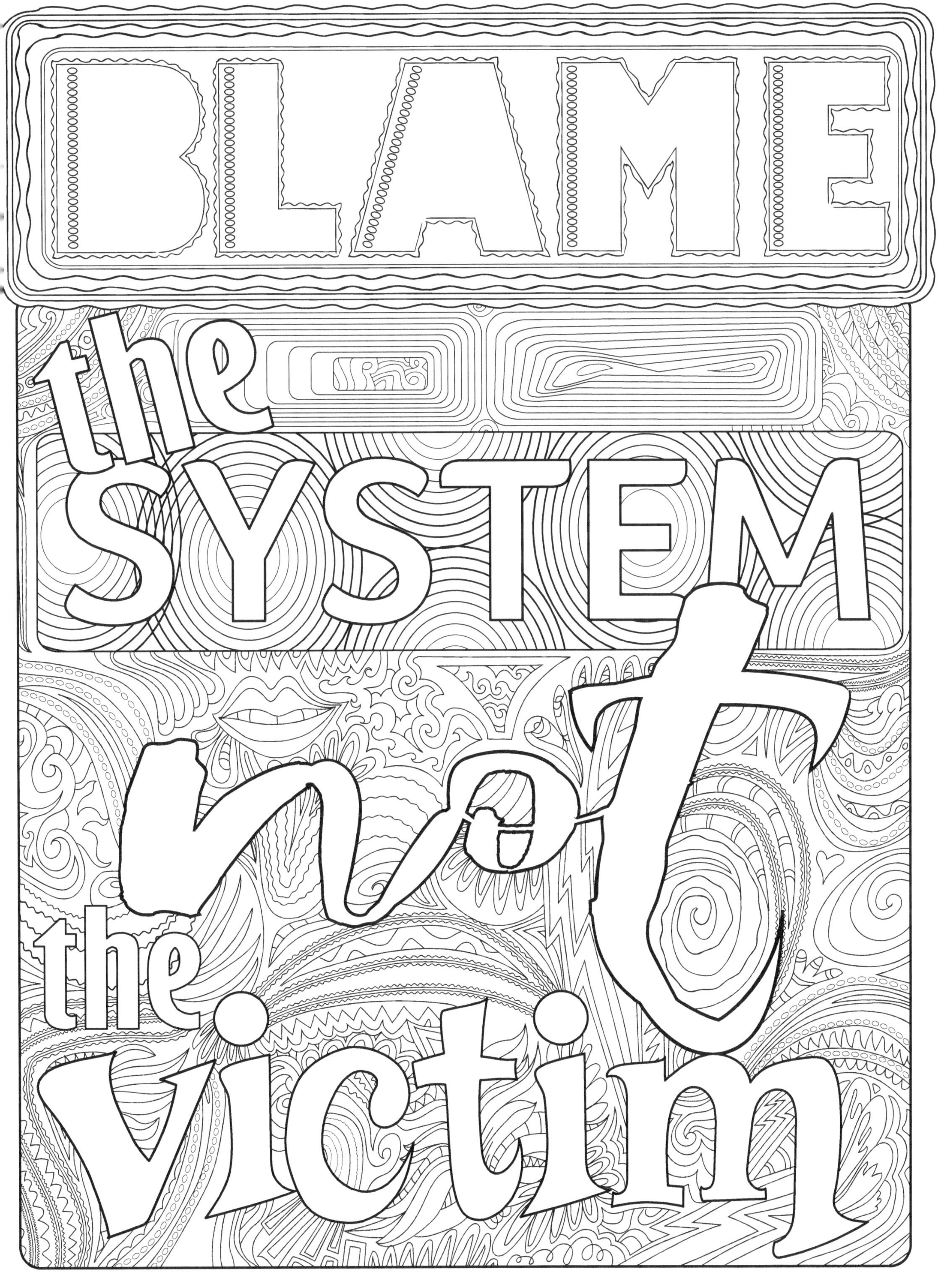

BLAME
the SYSTEM
not
the victim

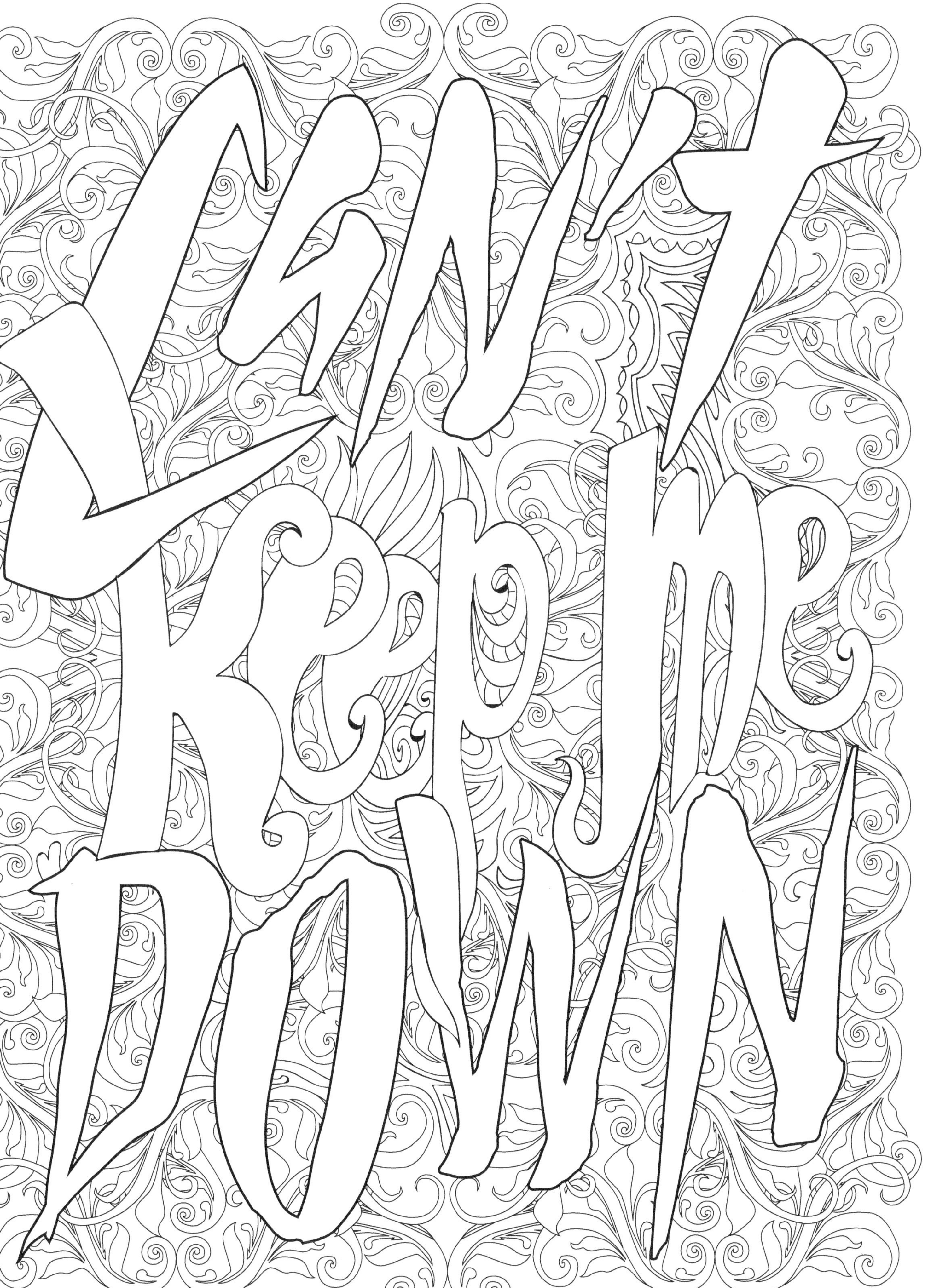
Can't
Keep Me
Down

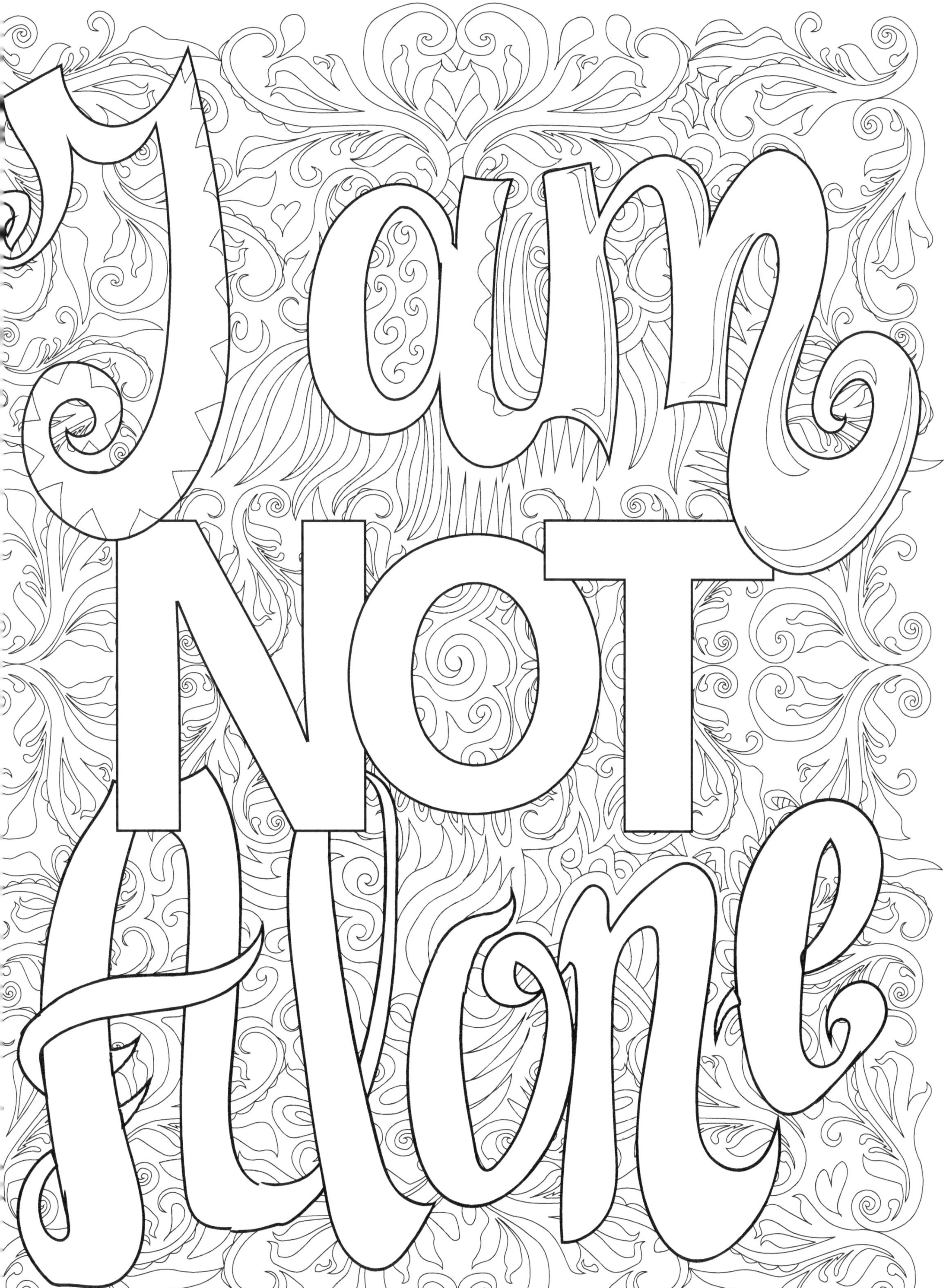
I am NOT Alone

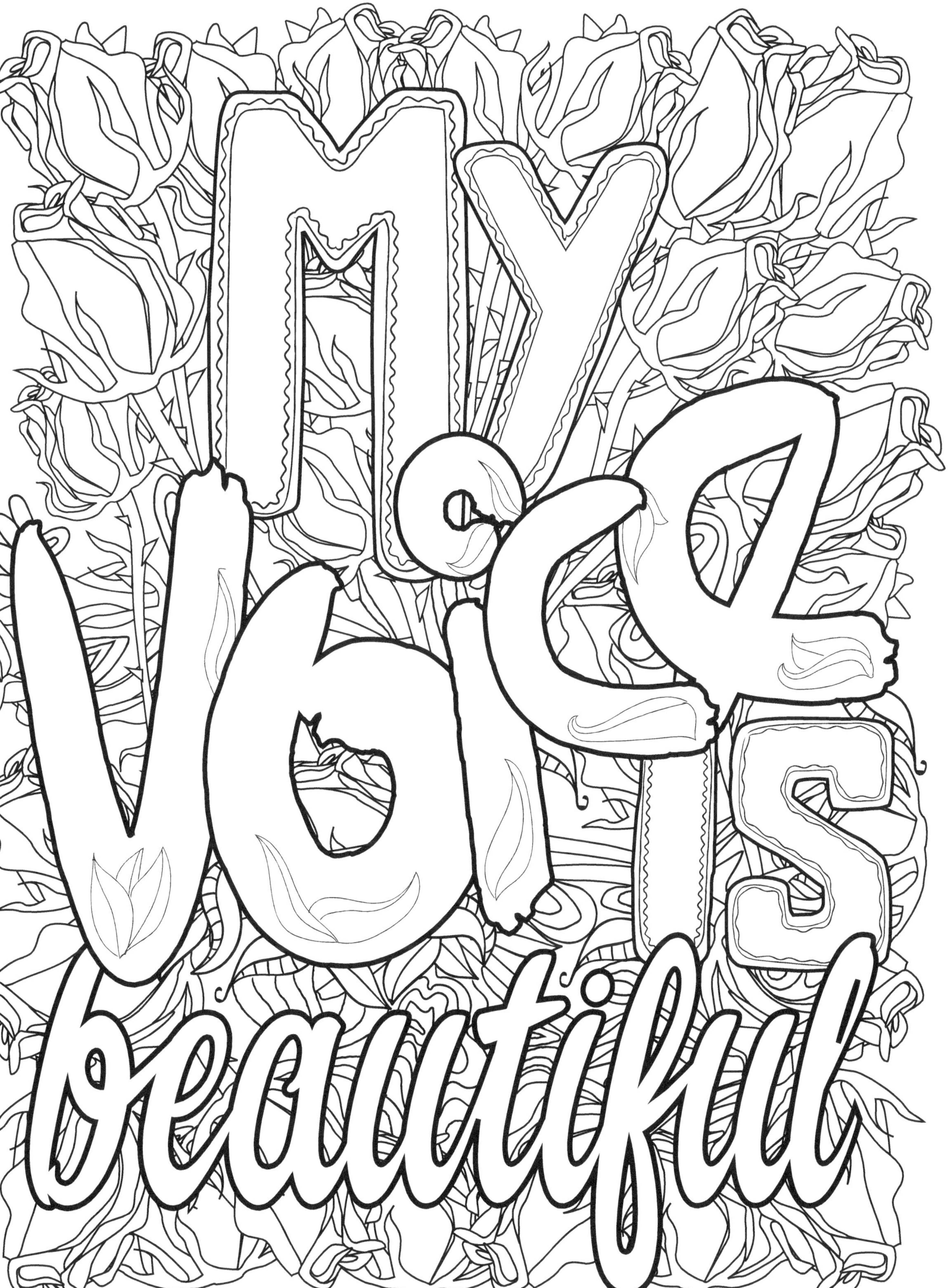
My
voice
is
beautiful

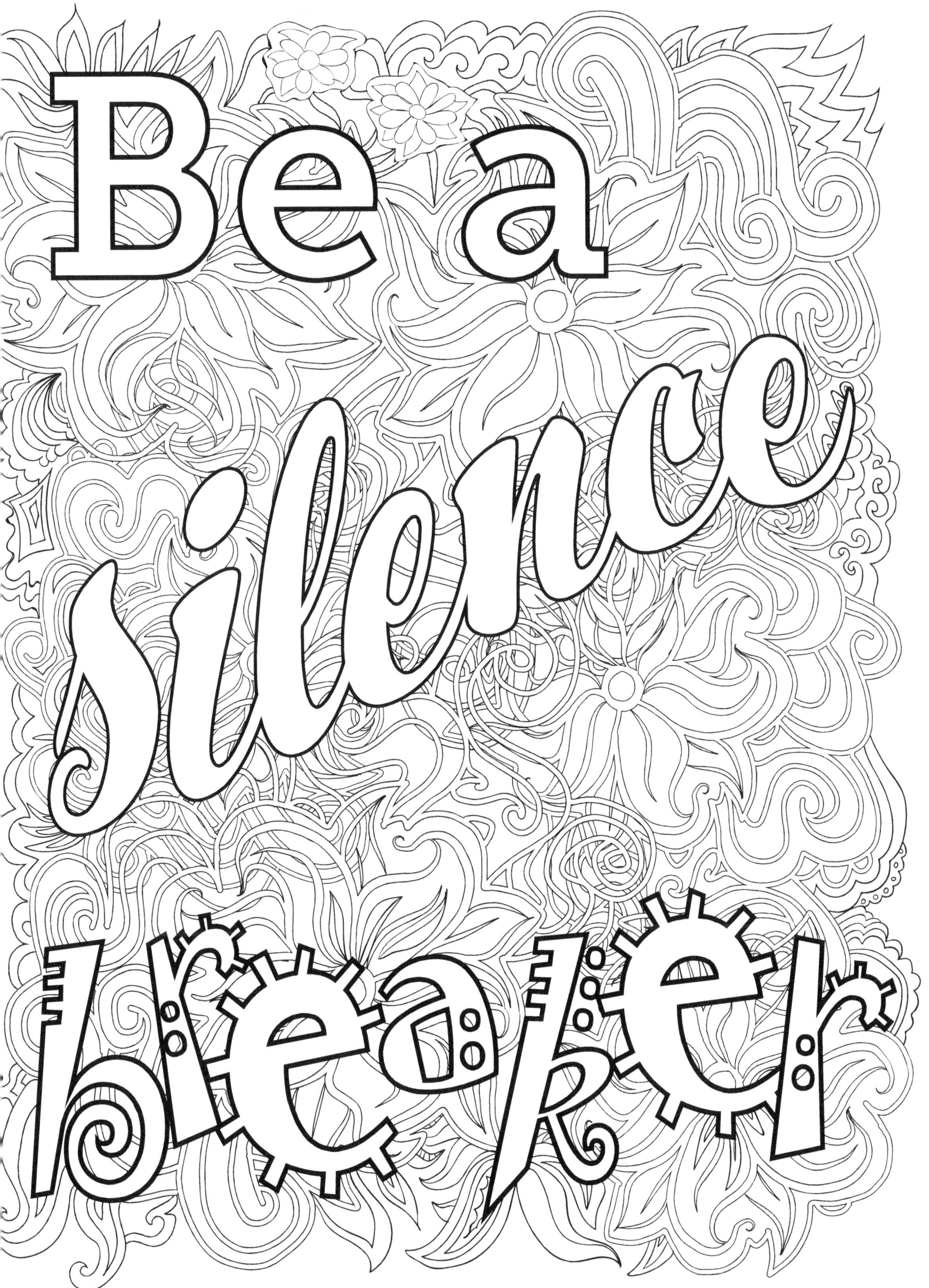
Be a
silence
breaker

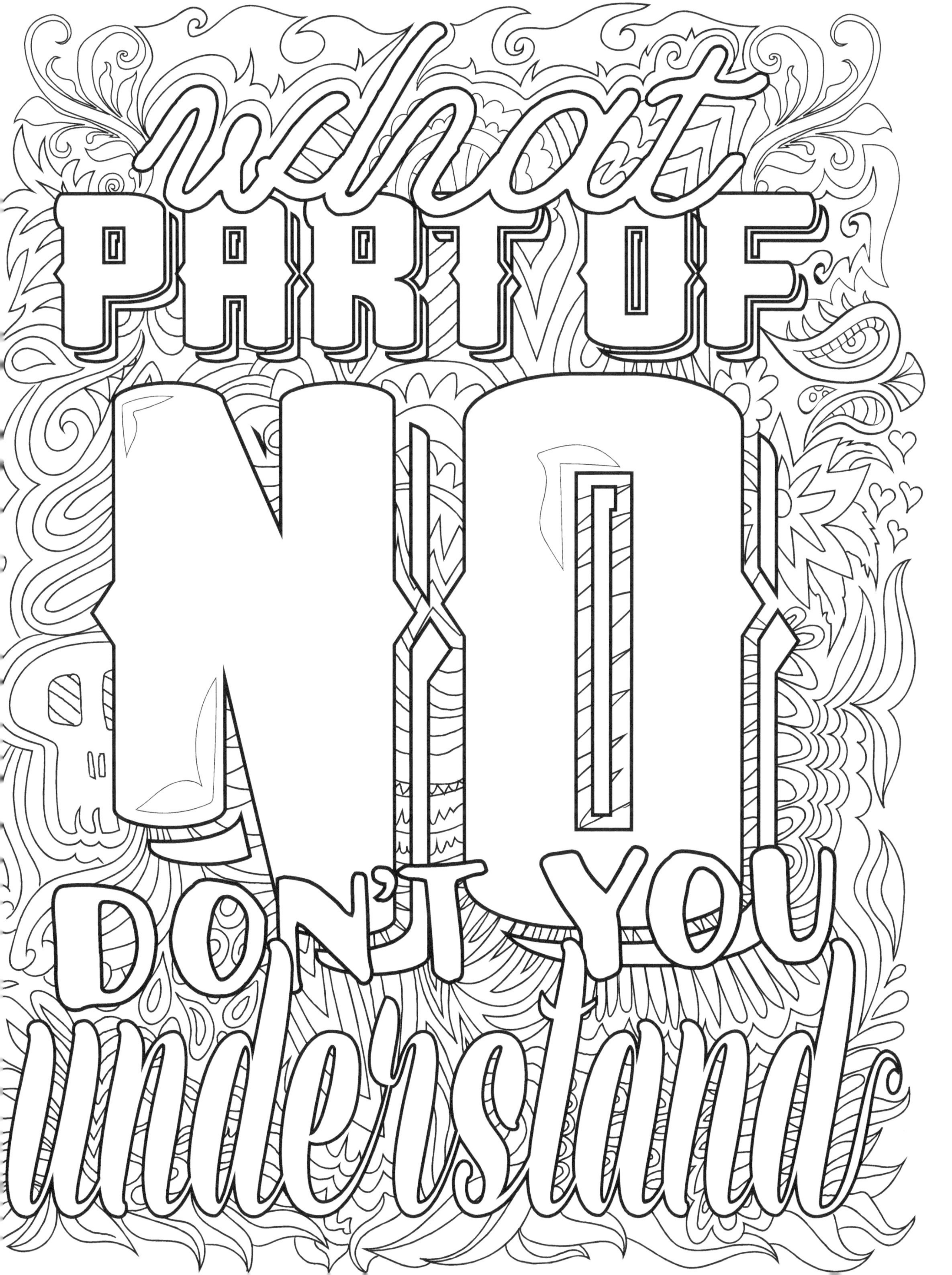
what
PART OF
NO
DON'T YOU
understand

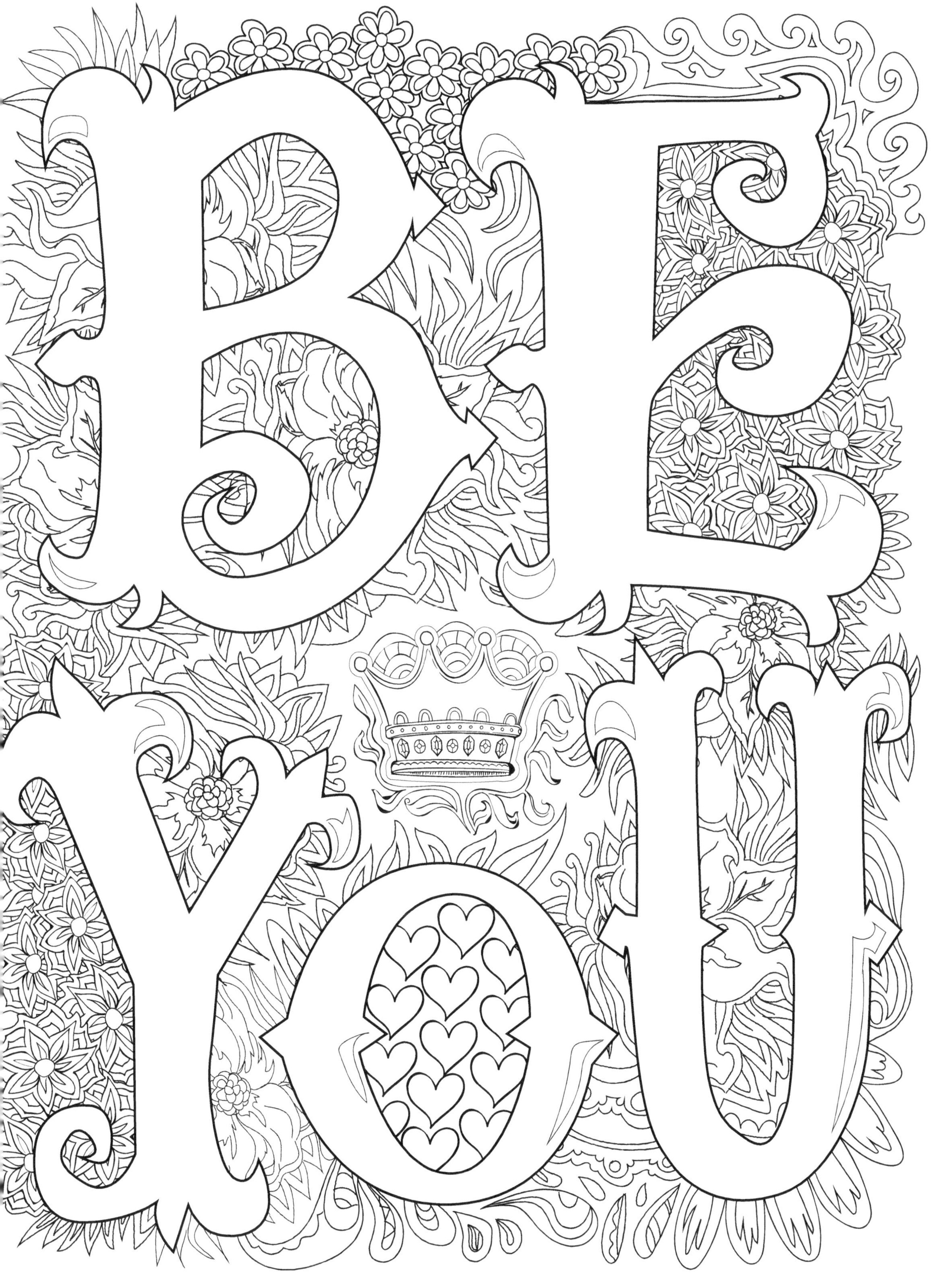
BE
YOU

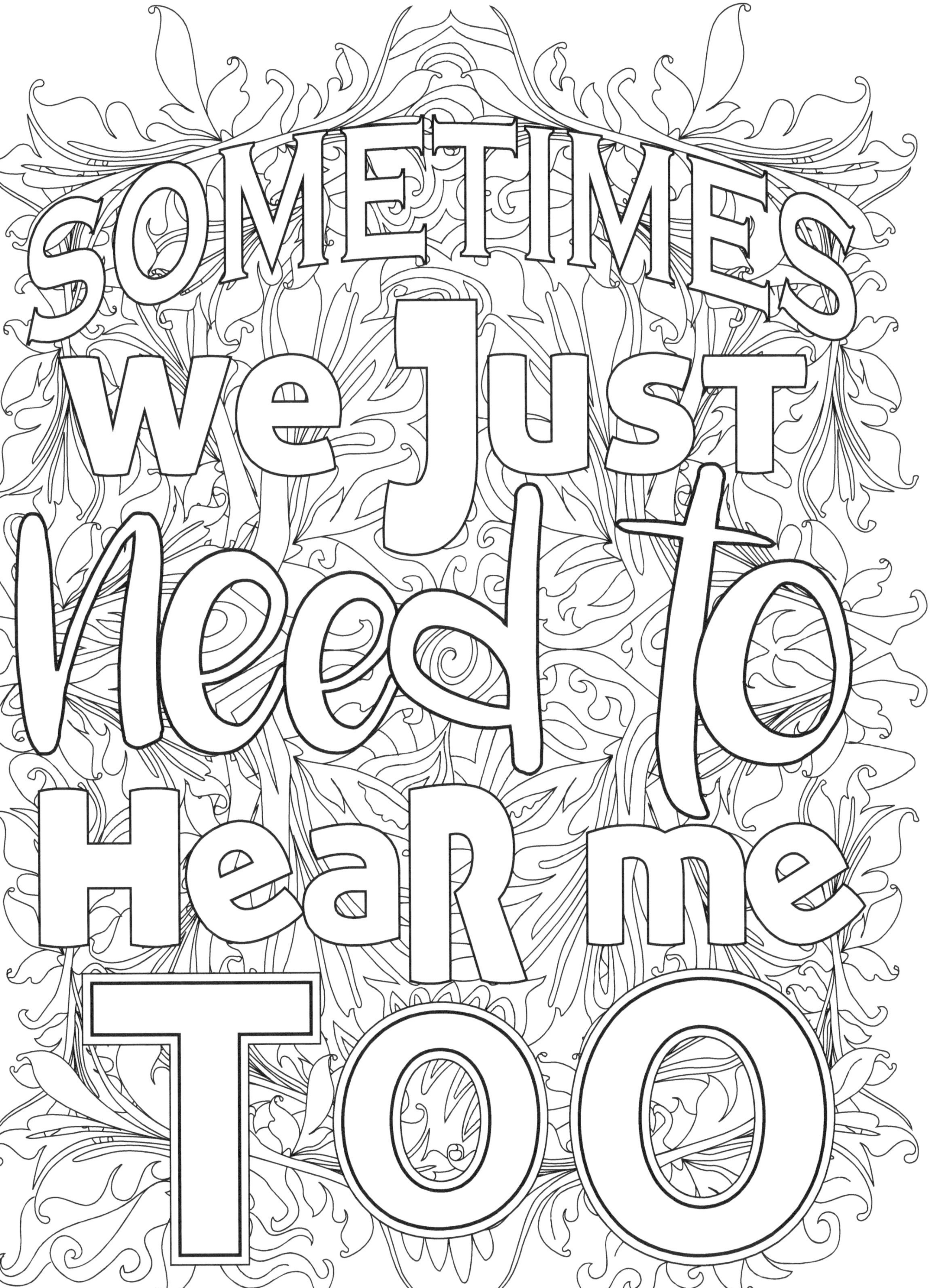
SOMETIMES
we Just
Need to
HeaR me
TOO

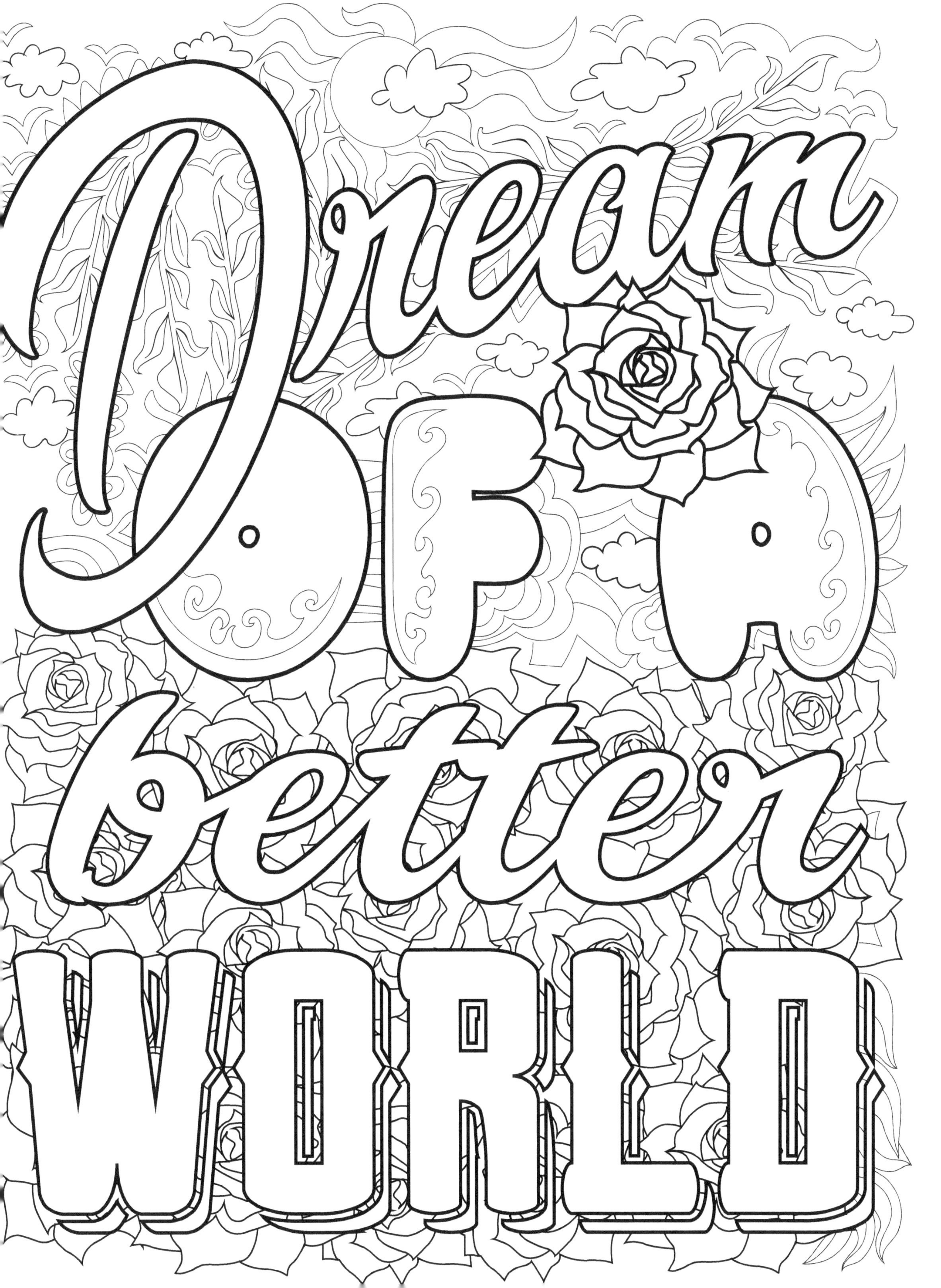
Dream
OF A
better
WORLD

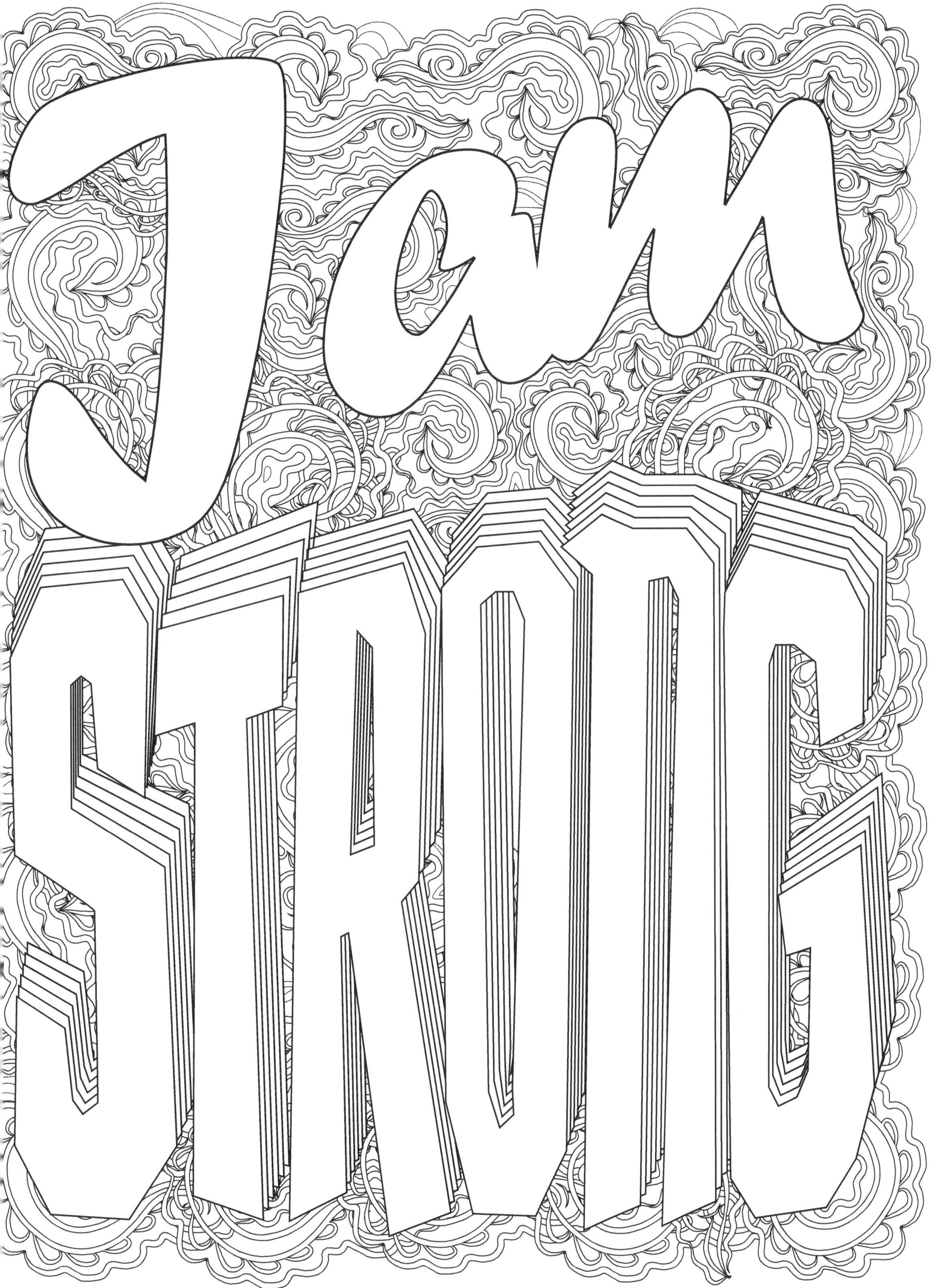
I am
STRONG

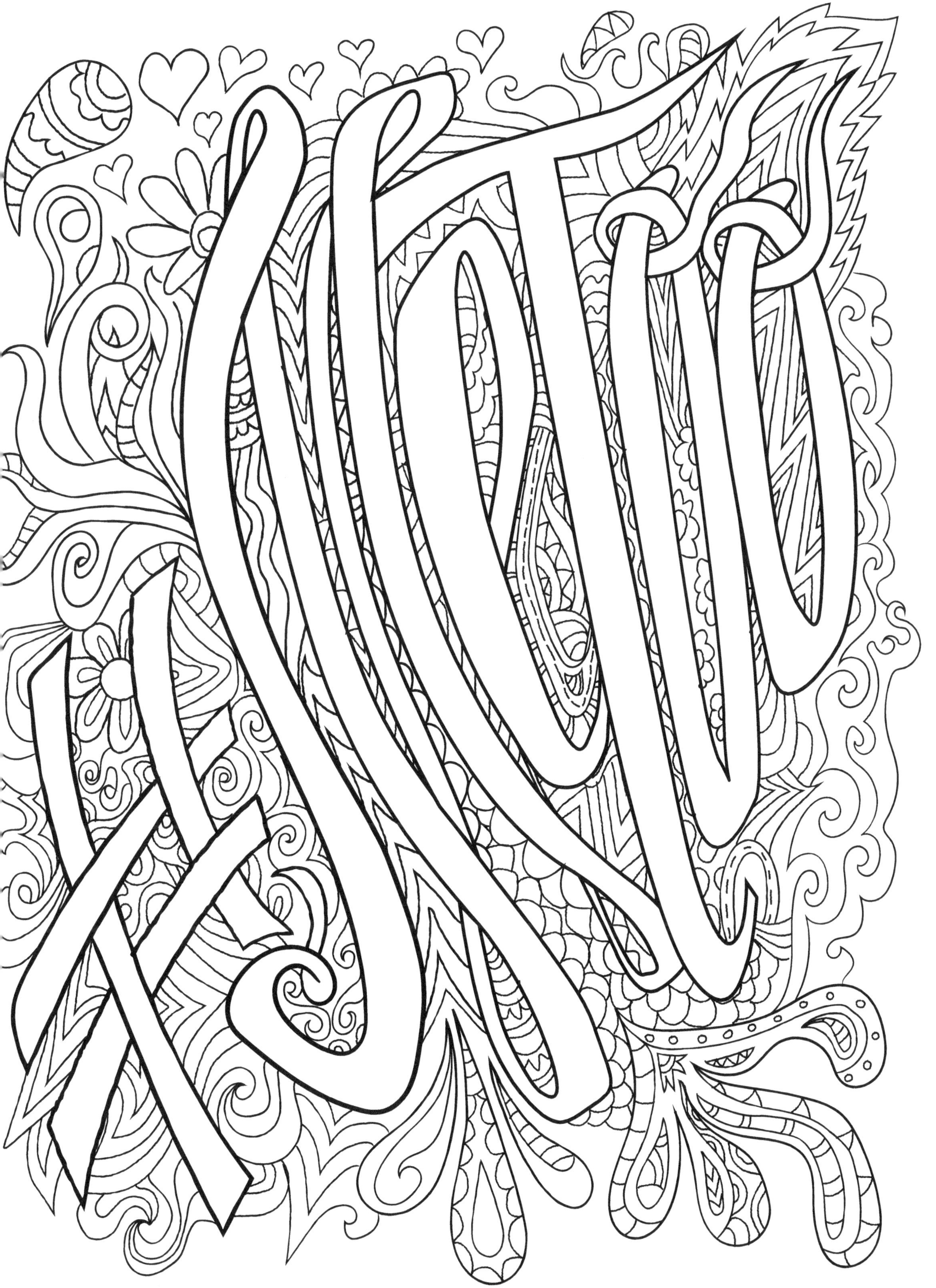

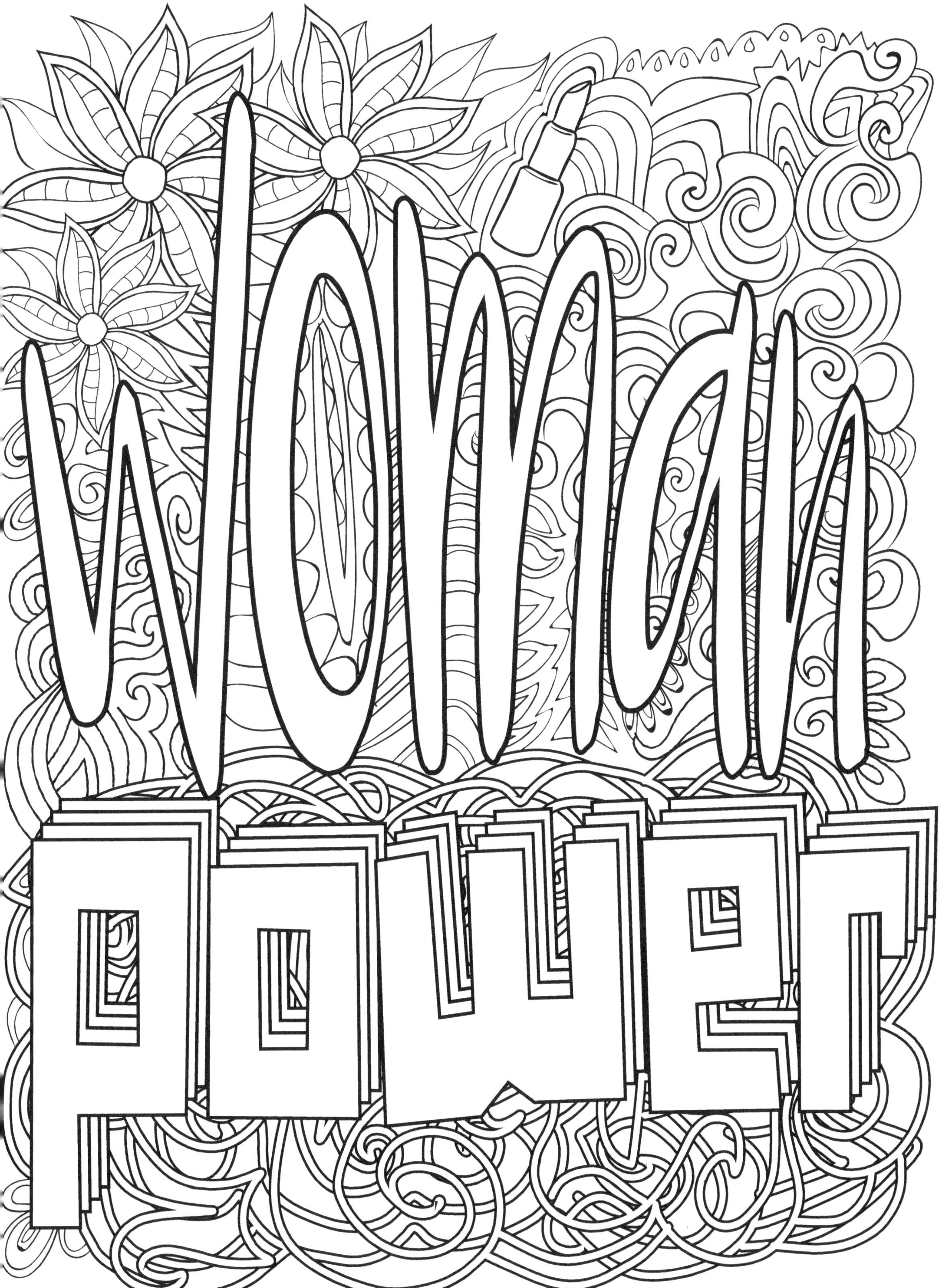
Woman
power

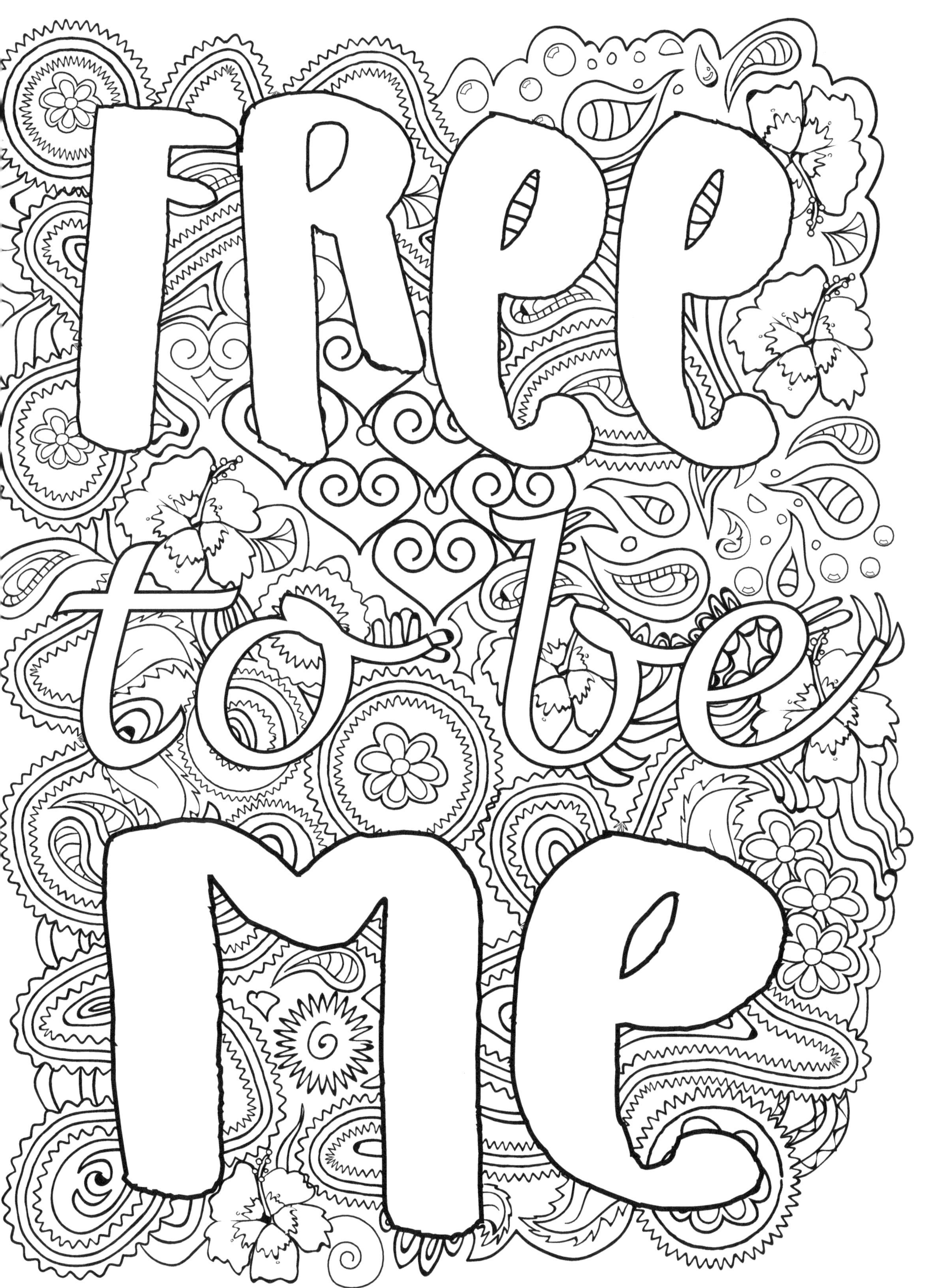
Free
to be
me

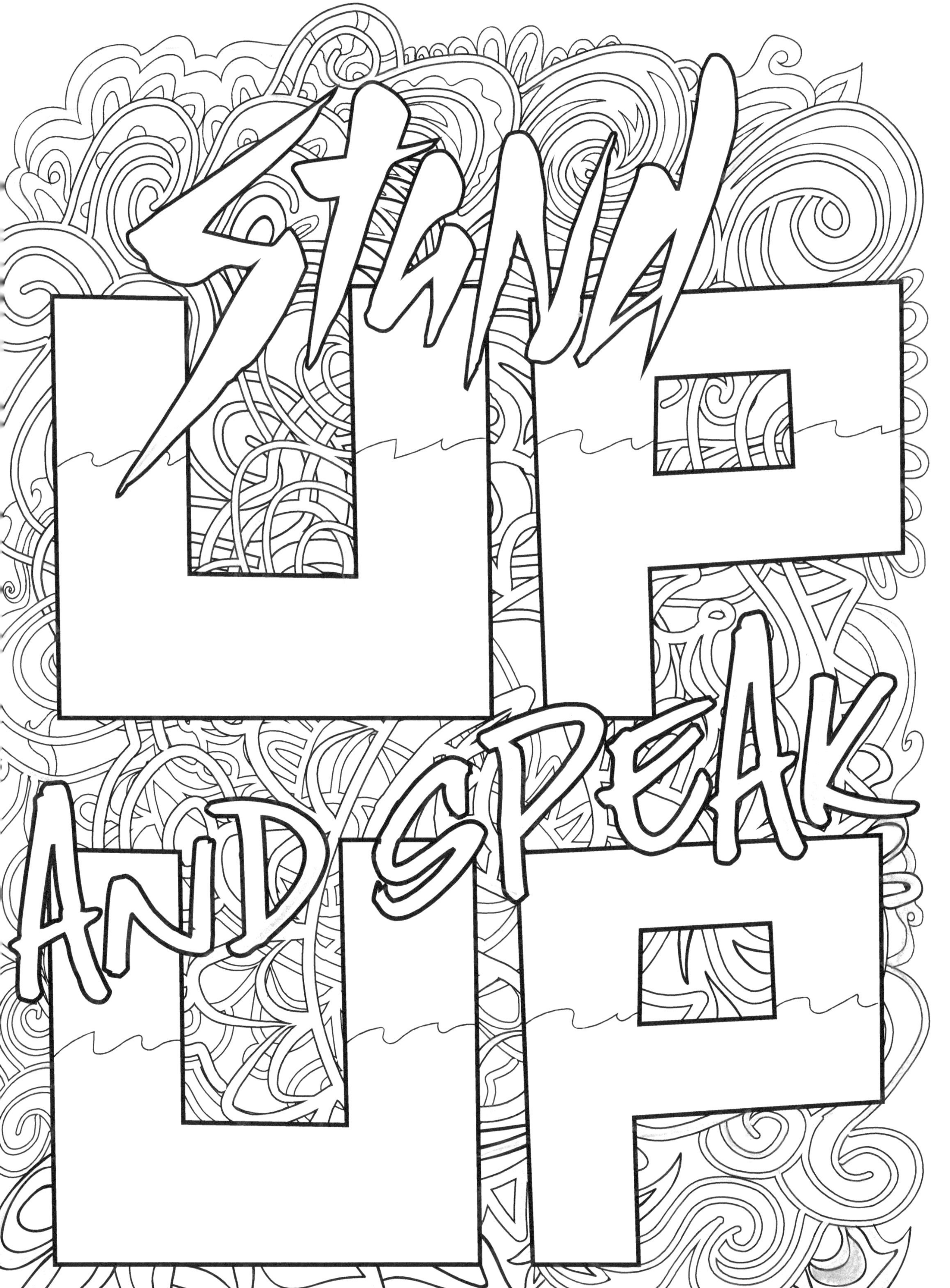
STAND
UP
AND SPEAK
UP

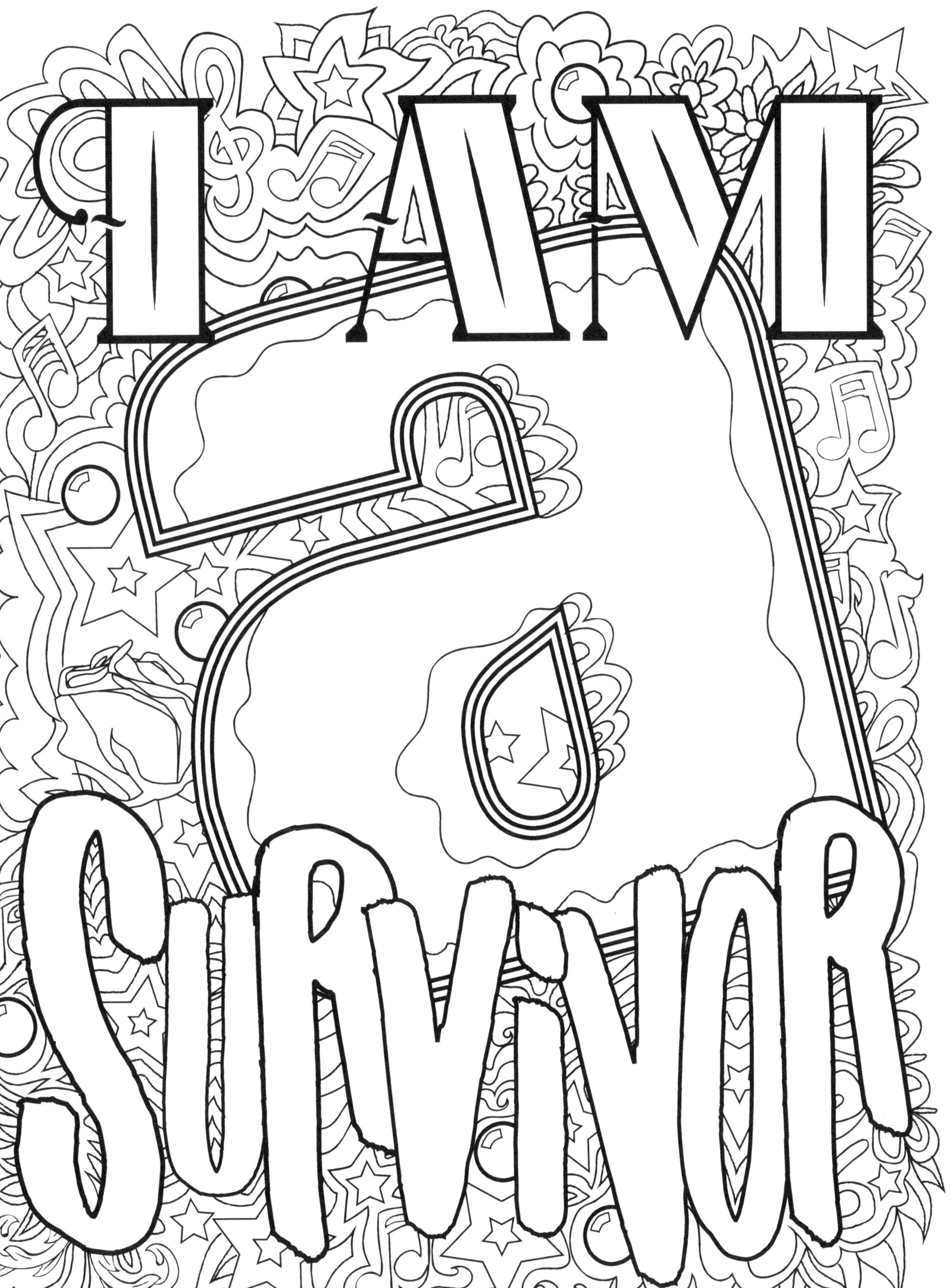
I AM
a
SURVIVOR

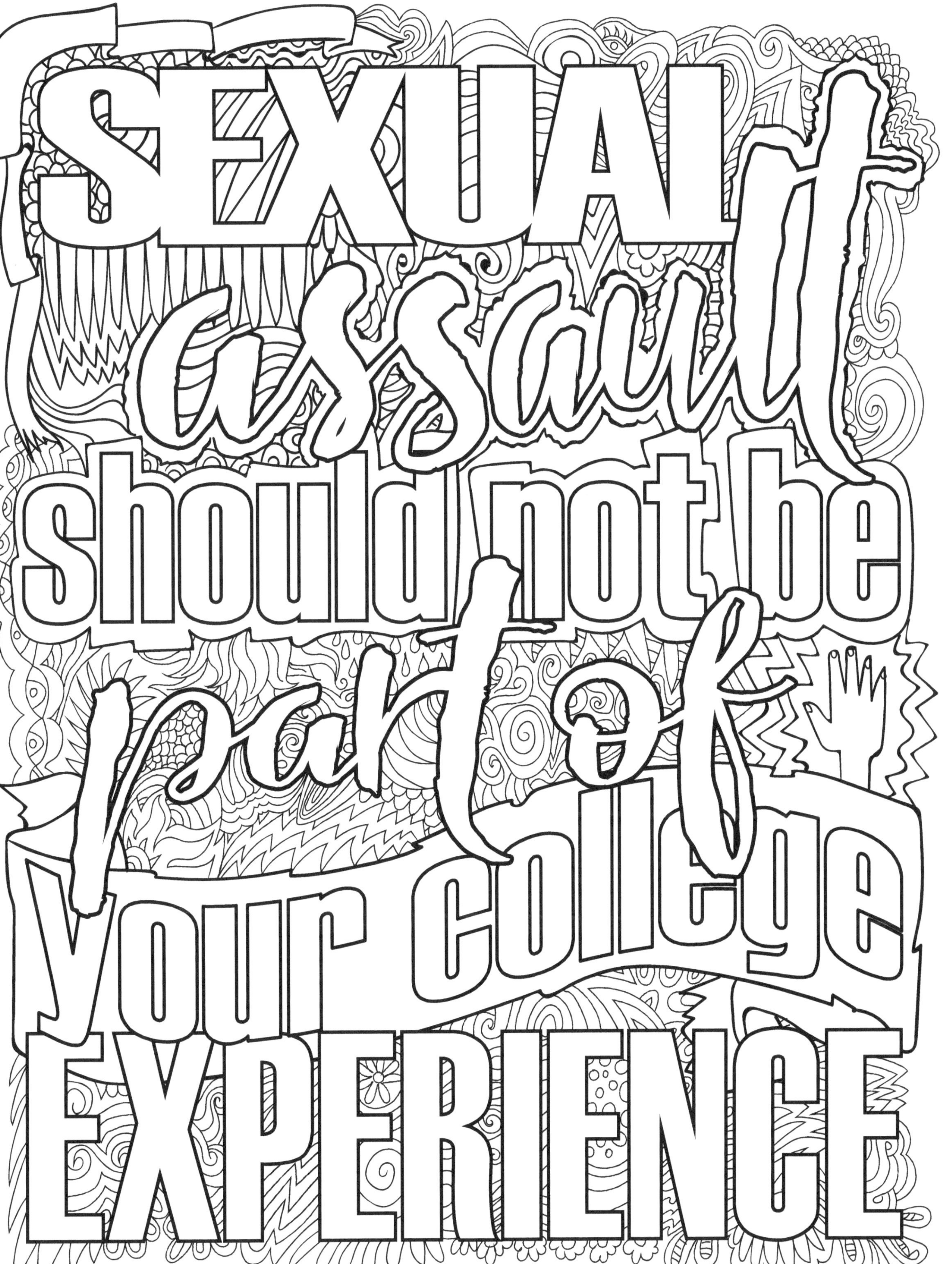
SEXUAL
assault
should not be
part of
your college
EXPERIENCE

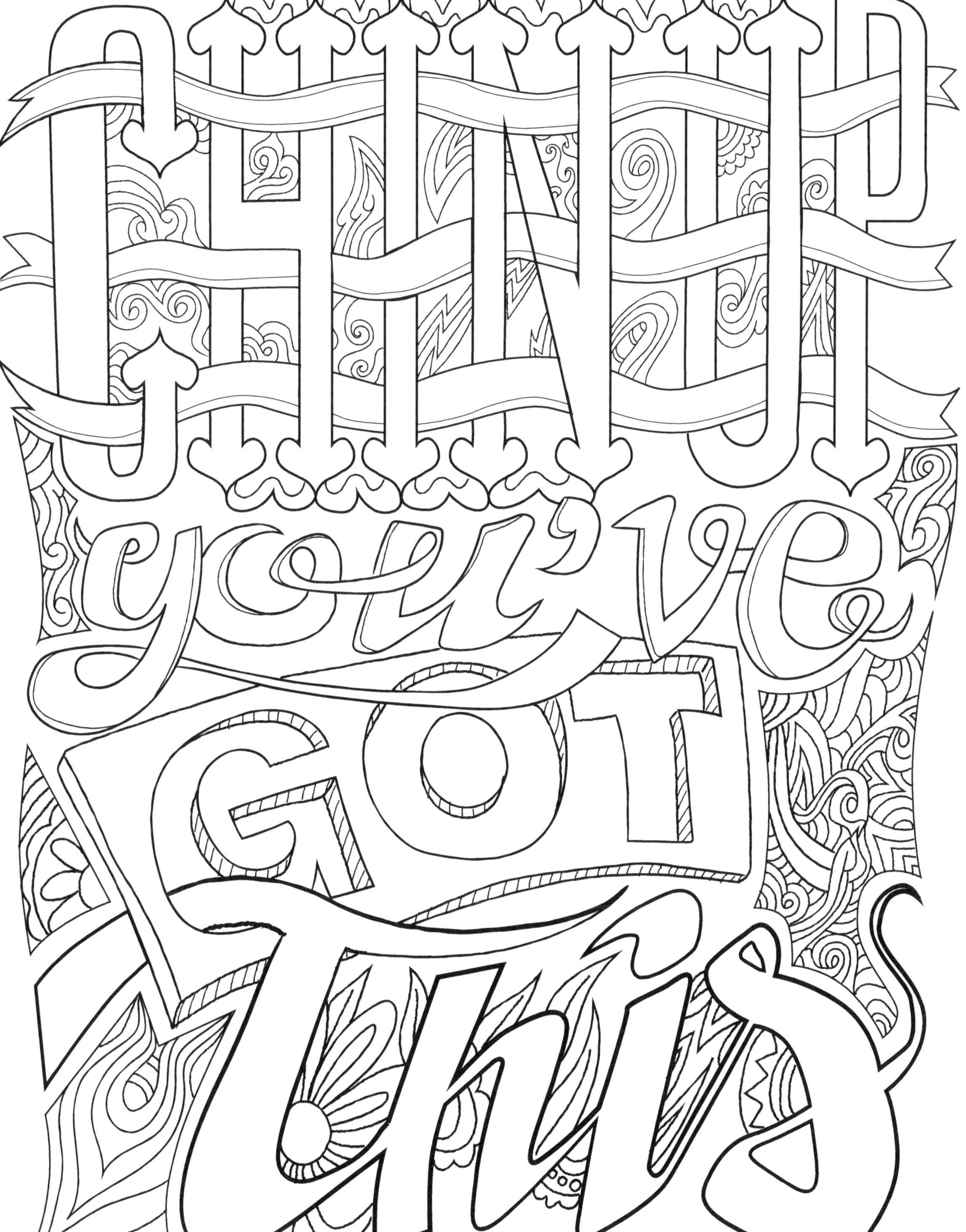
CHIN UP
you've
GOT
this

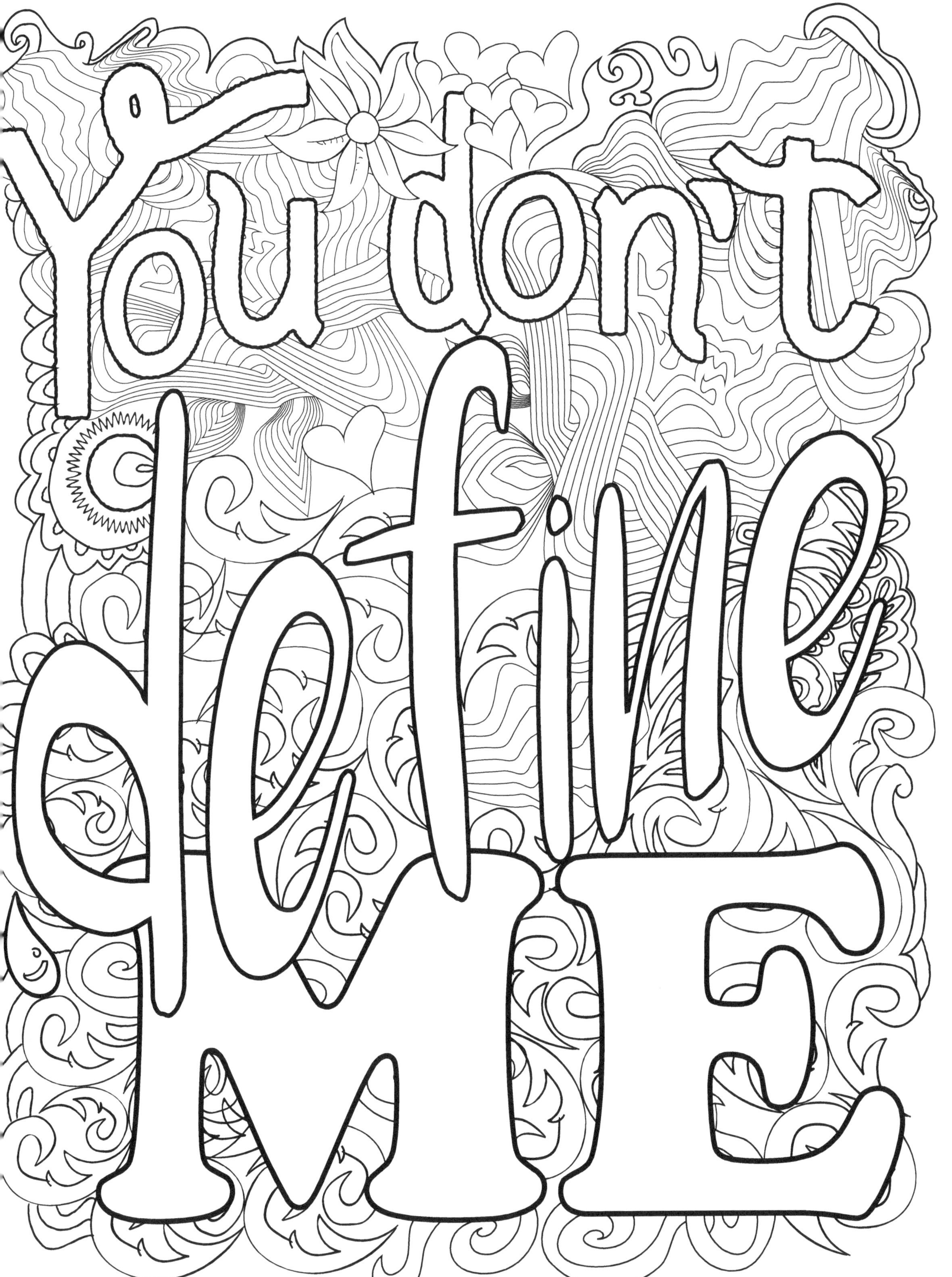
You don't
define
ME

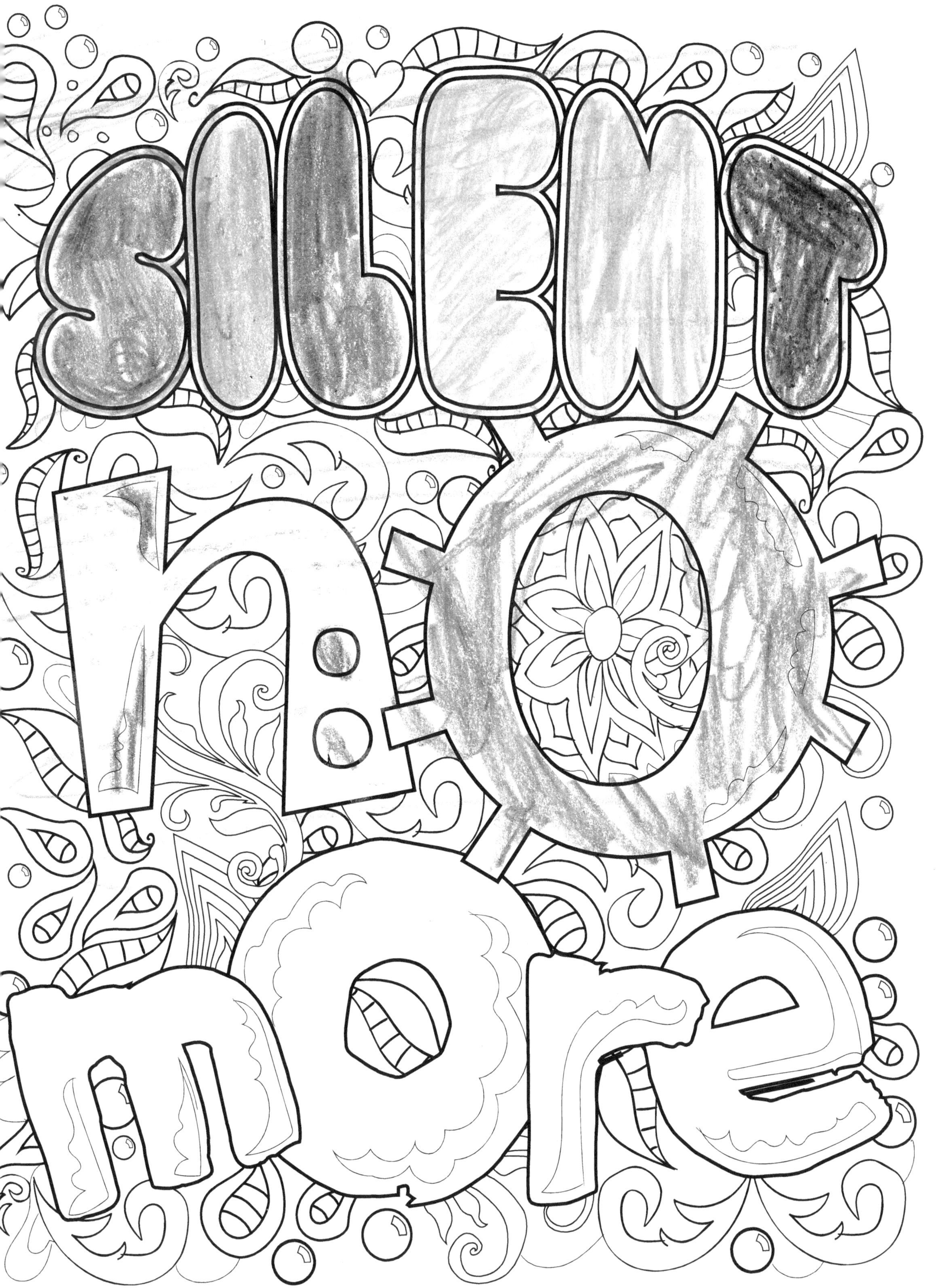
SILENT
no
more

CPSIA information can be obtained
at www.ICGtesting.com
Printed in the USA
LVHW101524240119
605132LV00015B/350/P

9 781945 056451